born in Dublin in 1971, Conor McPherson attended University College Dublin, where he began to write and direct. He co-founded the Fly by Night Theatre Company, which performed new plays in Dublin's fringe venues.

Published plays include *Rum and Vodka* (University College Dublin, 1992; Fly by Night, 1994); *The Good Thief* (Fly by Night, 1994; Stewart Parker Award); *This Lime Tree Bower* (Fly by Night, 1995; Bush Theatre, London, 1996); Thames TV, Guinness/National Theatre Ingenuity, and Meyer-Whitworth Awards); *St Nicholas* (Bush, 1997); *The Weir* (Royal Court, London, 1997; Broadway, New York, 1998; Olivier Best Play, Evening Standard and Critics' Circle Most Promising Playwright Awards); *Dublin Carol* (Royal Court, 2000); *Port Authority* (New Ambassadors, London; Gate Theatre, Dublin, 2001); *Come On Over* (Gate, 2001); and *Shining City* (Royal Court, 2004; Broadway, New York, 2006; Tony Award nomination, 2006).

Screenplays include *I Went Down*, *Saltwater* and *The Actors*, the last two of which he also directed.

Conor McPherson lives in Dublin.

Other titles in this Series

Conor McPherson

THE SEAFARER

NICK HERN BOOKS

London

www.nickhernbooks.co.uk

A Nick Hern Book

The Seafarer first published in Great Britain as a paperback original in 2006 by Nick Hern Books Limited, 14 Larden Road, London W3 7ST

The Seafarer copyright © 2006 Conor McPherson

Conor McPherson has asserted his right to be identified as the author of this work

Front cover image: design and photograph by Fionnuala Ní Chiosáin.

Cover by Ned Hoste, 2H

Typeset by Country Setting, Kingsdown, Kent CT14 8ES
Printed in Great Britain by Bookmarque, Croydon, Surrey

A CIP catalogue record for this book is available from the British Library

ISBN-13   978 1 85459 949 0
ISBN-10   1 85459 949 6

The Seafarer was first performed in the Cottesloe auditorium of the National Theatre, London, on 28 September 2006 (previews from 20 September), with the following cast:

MR LOCKHART   Ron Cook
IVAN CURRY   Conleth Hill
JAMES 'SHARKY' HARKIN   Karl Johnson
NICKY GIBLIN   Michael McElhatton
RICHARD HARKIN   Jim Norton

Director   Conor McPherson
Designer   Rae Smith
Lighting   Neil Austin
Sound   Mathew Smethurst-Evans

THE SEAFARER

Conor McPherson

> *He knows not*
> *Who lives most easily on land, how I*
> *Have spent my winter on the ice-cold sea*
> *Wretched and anxious, in the paths of exile*
> *Lacking dear friends, hung round by icicles*
> *While hail flew past in showers . . .*

Anonymous. *The Seafarer,* c.755 AD,
translated from Anglo-Saxon by Richard Hamer

Characters

JAMES 'SHARKY' HARKIN, *erstwhile fisherman/van driver/chauffeur, fifties*

RICHARD HARKIN, *his older brother, recently gone blind, late fifties/sixties*

IVAN CURRY, *old friend of the Harkins, late forties*

NICKY GIBLIN, *a friend of Richard's, late forties/fifties*

MR LOCKHART, *an acquaintance of Nicky's, fifties*

Setting

The action takes place in a house in Baldoyle, a coastal settlement north of Dublin City. It is an old area which could hardly be called a town these days. It is rather a suburb of the city with a church and a few pubs and shops at its heart. From the coast one is looking at the north side of the Howth peninsula. Howth Head (Binn Eadair) is a hill on the peninsula which marks the northern arm of Dublin Bay. Due to its prominence it has long been the focus of myths and legends.

Act One takes place on Christmas Eve morning and late afternoon.

Act Two takes place late on Christmas Eve night.

This text went to press before the end of rehearsals so may differ slightly from the play as performed.

ACT ONE: THE DEVIL AT BINN EADAIR

Scene One

The grim living area of a house in Baldoyle in Dublin. The house seems to be built into a hill. The main entrance is down a flight of stairs from the ground floor, giving a basement feel to the room. There is a window with a net curtain and threadbare heavier curtains drawn over it. At the back wall is an opening to a passageway giving access to a yard. Off the passageway are a mostly unseen kitchen and a toilet.

The place lacks a woman's touch. It has morphed into a kind of a bar in its appearance. Those who live or pass through here are so immersed in pub culture that many artefacts in the room are originally from bars: a big mirror advertising whiskey, ashtrays, beer mats, a bar stool or two somewhere. There is a cold stove. The furniture is old and worn. An armchair, a couch, mismatched chairs, a dresser with very old mugs, cups and various chipped plates, a little table more suited for playing cards than for eating at . . .

As the play begins the room is more or less in darkness. Some light seeps through from the kitchen, from the door to the yard, from down the stairs and through the threadbare curtains. There doesn't appear to be anyone here. An old stereo plays low music. A scrawny artificial Christmas tree haunts a corner.

SHARKY *comes down the stairs, pausing to tap a red light under a picture of the Sacred Heart which has gone out. It flickers to life for a second but goes out again as he descends and surveys the scene. He is in mismatched pyjamas with a sweater over them and wears a pair of runners. He is not a big man, but is wiry and strong. A very tough life is etched on his face. His eyes are quick and ready. He has a small plaster at the bridge of his nose and a few plasters on the knuckles of his right hand. He opens the curtains to let in the morning light which reveals the squalor. He goes to the stereo and shuts it off. He then realises the phone is ringing. He lifts the receiver.*

SHARKY. Hello? Hello?

He hangs up. As he does so, RICHARD, *his older brother, stirs awake. He has been asleep (passed out) on the floor where we didn't notice him or took him for a bundle of rags. He wears a black suit, one slipper, an ancient baseball cap and a filthy white shirt. He is unshaven and looks terrible. He has recently gone blind. He rises up behind* SHARKY . . .

RICHARD. Who's that? Sharky?

SHARKY (*startled*). What are you fucking doing?!

RICHARD. What happened?

SHARKY. Nothing – I just turned off the radio. I thought you told me you'd go up to bed!

RICHARD. Yeah, I meant to, but I'd no one to help me up the stairs!

SHARKY. Where was Ivan?

RICHARD. I don't know! He must've gone home.

SHARKY. I thought you said you could feel your way up!

RICHARD. Ah, Sharky! Not when I'm jarred!

SHARKY (*going to* RICHARD, *picking up a slipper*). For fuck's sake, Richard . . .

RICHARD. Ah, don't be at me now, I'm not able for it. What time is it?

SHARKY. It's half ten.

RICHARD. Oh God, I'm bursting . . . give us a hand, where's me stick?

SHARKY, *slipper in hand, looks around for* RICHARD'*s stick, while* RICHARD *shakily holds on to the chair, one slipper on, one slipper off.*

Sharky!

SHARKY. I'm here!

RICHARD. God, it's freezing! Where's me stick?

SHARKY. I don't know! Where did you put it?

RICHARD. If I knew where I put it, I'd have it!

SHARKY. Ah, don't fucking start, I'm looking for it, if you'd've let me bring you up to bed last night you'd have everything . . .

RICHARD. Ivan was here! What was I gonna do, leave him sitting in here on his own?

SHARKY. No, you were too busy drinking your fucking brains out.

SHARKY *goes towards the kitchen.*

RICHARD. Hark at you! Hark at Sharky! That's a good one! 'The hypocrite's voice haunts his own den!'

SHARKY *returns with the stick.*

SHARKY. Here, I have it.

RICHARD. Where was it?

SHARKY. It was outside the jacks door. Where it was yesterday as well.

SHARKY *gives* RICHARD *the stick and crouches to help* RICHARD *get his slipper on.*

RICHARD. Would you give me a hand and bring me through!!

SHARKY. I am! What do you think I'm doing?

SHARKY *lifts* RICHARD'*s foot into his slipper.*

RICHARD. Alright! I'm just asking . . . Jaysus, who got out of bed on the wrong side this morning?

SHARKY (*helping* RICHARD *towards the passageway*). Good fuck, Richard, you absolutely stink again, do you know that?

RICHARD. Yeah, happy Christmas to you as well!

SHARKY. Would you not let me put you in the bath? I'll give you a nice shave.

RICHARD. I told you! Tomorrow! Christmas morning! What's the point doing it today? I'll only stink the place out for Santy!

SHARKY. Alright! Relax! You have me going deaf in that ear!

SHARKY opens the toilet door.

Ah, Richard, who did that all over the floor?

RICHARD. Well, I don't know!

SHARKY. Come on, let me bring you upstairs I'll give you a shave, come on.

RICHARD. I said tomorrow! Would you let me do my toilet please, Sharky? For . . . Jaysus' sake will you come out of me road?

SHARKY (*off*). I am! Let me just wipe the seat . . .

RICHARD (*storming in and ejecting* SHARKY). Come out of me road!

The toilet door slams. SHARKY *tidies up a few things, finding a bottle of Powers whiskey under a chair with about a quarter left. He goes to the stove and pokes around in there.*

(*Off.*) Sharky!

SHARKY. What?

RICHARD (*off*). Is there not any jacks roll in here?

SHARKY. I don't know! You're in there!

RICHARD (*off*). Well there's none on the holder and I can't feel on the floor . . .

SHARKY. Hold on!

SHARKY goes into the kitchen and takes a roll of tissue paper to the toilet.

RICHARD (*off*). Don't come in!

SHARKY. Well what do you want me to do?

RICHARD (*off*). Just hand me in some!

SHARKY. There's only kitchen roll here, okay?

RICHARD (*off*). Just hand it in to me.

SHARKY. Here . . .

RICHARD (*off*). Where's your hand?

SHARKY. Here! Here!

> SHARKY *slams the toilet door.*

RICHARD (*off*). Don't slam the door!

> SHARKY *reappears and begins laying the table for some breakfast, bringing out a bowl of mandarin oranges, and a Kellogg's variety pack of various cereals in small boxes. He goes back into the kitchen. IVAN appears at the top of the stairs. He is a big burly man with a red face and curly hair. He wears a shirt tucked into his pants, the back sticking out. He feels his way gingerly down. SHARKY comes back with some milk and two bowls.*

IVAN (*sheepishly*). Morning, Sharky.

SHARKY. Ivan! Did you stay over?

IVAN. Yeah, no, I couldn't get a taxi. (*Hands shaking . . .*) Oh God, I feel terrible.

SHARKY. Have some breakfast.

IVAN. Oh God, I don't know. Let me just . . . get my bearings for a minute, is that okay?

SHARKY. You don't have to ask me that, Ivan. Sure, do whatever you . . .

IVAN. Yeah, no, I . . . can't find my glasses. You didn't see them?

SHARKY (*looking*). Em . . . Where did you . . . did you get a good kip?

IVAN. Yeah, yeah . . . I was dead to the world just then. What was all the shouting?

SHARKY. Ah, that was . . . (*He signals 'Richard'*.)

IVAN. When did you get back?

SHARKY. I got back three . . . four days ago.

IVAN. Yeah?

SHARKY. Sure, I was talking to you last night!

IVAN. Were you here last night?

SHARKY. Yeah, I made yous hot whiskeys . . .

IVAN. Oh yeah . . .

SHARKY. Do you not remember?

IVAN. No yeah, no, no I do. Just I wasn't even . . . sure I was only on my way home. I was only calling in to see if your man was alright . . . I certainly didn't mean to still fucking be here! Jaysus . . .

SHARKY (*laughs*). Yeah, well . . . Listen, thanks for all the . . . calling in on him and . . . he's . . . eh . . .

IVAN. Yeah, yeah, no, no bother. God, I'm gonna be killed . . .

SHARKY. Are you?

IVAN. No, there's still a few Christmas bits I have to do. God, I'm gonna be killed now.

SHARKY. How is Karen keeping?

IVAN. Don't talk to me.

SHARKY. Yeah?

IVAN. Don't talk to me.

SHARKY. And the kids?

IVAN. Ah, they're great, yeah. They're grand, you know yourself.

SHARKY. Yeah, well that's . . .

IVAN. Yeah . . .

Pause.

SHARKY (*calling off*). Are you alright there, Rich?

RICHARD (*off*). What's wrong with ya?

SHARKY. No, I was just seeing if you were alright?

RICHARD (*off*). Would you leave me alone? I'm trying to go to the fucking toilet in here!

SHARKY. I'll just grab the . . . the tea . . .

IVAN. Yeah, yeah, work away.

SHARKY *goes into the kitchen.* IVAN *moves through the room a little, throwing his eye around quickly for something to drink. He can't see anything.* SHARKY *comes back with a pot of tea and some cups then he goes to put some briquettes in the stove.*

SHARKY. Here, were yous out the back last night?

IVAN. What? Oh! Yeah . . . Oh no, it was . . . (*Unsaid 'stupid'.*) Did you hear him?

SHARKY. Ah yeah, I heard him, I heard yous. I rolled over, I tried to just ignore it. Sure that's . . .

IVAN. Yeah . . .

SHARKY. . . . that's a regular . . .

IVAN. I know, mad!

SHARKY. What was it? The winos out in the lane?

IVAN. Yeah! We were sitting there at the fire and bang! Suddenly he gets up! I'm like, 'What are you doing?' He's like, 'Them winos are out in the lane again! I'm gonna kill them!' he says, waving the fucking . . . stick around!

SHARKY. I know!

IVAN. Nearly took my fucking head off with it, and out he runs, *off* on out through the back there, it was nearly like he could see! You know?

SHARKY. I know!

IVAN (*rubbing his elbow gingerly*). And I . . . fucking went over, smack! . . . on them newspapers all in the back door there, trying to stop him! And then out in the garden or . . . ! I didn't know where I was!

SHARKY. I know. He's a mad bollocks, Ivan.

IVAN. Ah no, he's alright. He's just . . . (*Beat.*) So, here, did I ask you this last night? How did you get on down in . . . Where was this you were?

SHARKY. I was down in Lahinch, in County Clare.

IVAN. Yeah?

SHARKY. Yeah, it was, it was, it was . . . it was great.

IVAN. You got on well?

SHARKY. Yeah, got on great. Down the country is great, you know . . .

IVAN. Ah, down the country's smashing. Were you on the boats or . . . ?

SHARKY. Nah . . . Can't get a job on the boats. But the people I was working for were spot on . . .

IVAN. What were you doing? Chauffeur?

SHARKY. Yeah, I was doing a bit of driving for this developer guy . . . and his wife there and eh . . . (*Short pause.*) But I had to get back up because . . .

He signals 'Richard'. They hear an attempt to flush the toilet.

IVAN. Ah yeah, no, fair play, Sharky. Oh here, Nicky Giblin was telling me, how's the . . .

They stop to listen to RICHARD'*s attempts to flush the toilet.*

SHARKY (*calling*). Are you alright, Rich?

RICHARD (*off*). Ah, I can't flush this fucking thing!

SHARKY. Do you want me to do it?

RICHARD (*off*). Is that Ivan out there?

SHARKY. He's heard you.

IVAN (*going towards kitchen door*). Are you alright, Richard? Do you not want your brother?

RICHARD (*off*). No, Ivan, you're strong. Come here and give this yoke a yank, will ya?

IVAN *goes off to help* RICHARD. SHARKY *continues to get the breakfast and tidy up while* IVAN *and* RICHARD *attend to the toilet.*

(*Off.*) That's it – one more like that, Ivan . . .

IVAN (*off*). Here give us that till I stick it down the . . . hold on, come away . . .

The toilet flushes. IVAN *leads* RICHARD *back out.*

RICHARD. Well done, Ivan . . . sorry about that . . .

SHARKY. Lads, some breakfast.

IVAN (*unable to consider it*). Oh . . .

RICHARD. What is there?

SHARKY. There's toast, if you want, there's cereal . . .

RICHARD. What cereal?

SHARKY (*looking at variety pack*). There's Cornflakes, there's Frosties, there's Coco Pops, there's . . .

RICHARD (*gravely*). Em . . . Coco Pops . . .

SHARKY. Okay, and I've mandarin oranges, there's tea, Ivan.

RICHARD. Did you not get coffee?

SHARKY (*pouring out bowl of cereal*). No, I told you, I forgot, I'll get it today.

RICHARD. You know what I'd really like?

SHARKY. What?

RICHARD. Ivan? Irish coffee . . .

IVAN. Oh now . . .

RICHARD. Warm us up!

SHARKY. Yeah, well, we don't even have coffee so . . .

RICHARD. Well, then, we'll just have the Irish and no coffee
    – ha, Ivan?

SHARKY (*going to kitchen*). I'll put on some toast.

RICHARD. Well, Ivan, how's the head?

IVAN. Don't talk to me, Rich. I can't find my glasses. I'm like
    you, I'm feeling my way around.

RICHARD. Well they have to be here somewhere. Did you
    have them when you got here?

IVAN. I'm assuming I did.

    SHARKY *comes back.*

RICHARD (*of* SHARKY). Hey, check out Johnny Weismuller,
    off the drink for . . . what is it, Sharky? Two days?

SHARKY. What?

RICHARD. How long are you on the dry now? Two days, is
    it? I was just telling Ivan. The old delirium tremens must be
    fairly ramping up now, ha?

    SHARKY *ignores him.*

IVAN. Yeah well, fair play. Hey Shark, I was gonna ask you,
    how's the nose? Nicky Giblin was telling me.

    SHARKY *signals to him not to continue with this line of
    enquiry.* IVAN *doesn't twig it in time.*

RICHARD. What's this?

IVAN. Did he not tell you?

SHARKY (*signalling to* IVAN *who finally sees him*). No, it
    was nothing . . .

RICHARD. Tell me what?

Pause.

What? Tell me what?

IVAN. No . . . eh . . . Nicky was . . . (*Dismissively.*) Ah, you know Nicky . . .

RICHARD. I know Nicky well! What happened to you, Sharky?

SHARKY. Ah, it was nothing, it was . . .

RICHARD. What? Ivan?

IVAN. Ah . . . (*To* SHARKY.) Nicky was saying, I was only asking to see if you were . . . (*To* RICHARD.) Nicky was saying that Sharky got in a spot of bother there off someone there outside the Elphin and I was just . . .

RICHARD. When was this?

SHARKY. Ah, it was . . . it was the other evening . . . the night I got here.

RICHARD. You kept that very quiet! What happened?

SHARKY. Ah, it was fucking . . . I got off the Dart at Howth Junction and I was . . .

RICHARD. What did you get off at Howth Junction for?

SHARKY. Ah, I meant to go to Bayside or Sutton Cross, and I mixed it up and I . . .

RICHARD. You blew it!

SHARKY. Yeah, well I was walking all up there, up the coast, and . . .

RICHARD. Why didn't you get a taxi?

SHARKY. I had no cash!

RICHARD. Go on out of that, you were in the Elphin!

SHARKY. No, I went into the Elphin . . .

RICHARD (*sarcastically, as though he had failed to see a big distinction*). Oh!

SHARKY. I needed to make a phone call . . . my phone was . . .

RICHARD. Go on out of that! You were jarred from the train, you got off at the wrong fucking station . . .

SHARKY. I fucking . . . ! I had two, three pints . . . (*To* IVAN.) 'cause young Cathy Wolfe was having her birthday in there and her da bought me one . . .

RICHARD. Oh . . . I see . . .

SHARKY. And then the end of the match was on and . . .

RICHARD. Ah, of course . . .

SHARKY. Ah, I'm not gonna fucking tell you if you're . . .

RICHARD. No, I'm only having you on! What happened?

Pause.

SHARKY. Ah . . . I was coming out and there was some lads messing around, sitting on the bonnet of a car out there and . . .

Pause.

RICHARD. What happened?

SHARKY. Ah, I just said, 'Come up off of that . . . ' as I was kind of walking by . . .

RICHARD. What?

SHARKY. Just, only, not even that serious, you know . . .

RICHARD. You fucking eejit . . .

SHARKY. And next thing, I'm down at the corner, they're all around me! And your man is, 'What did you fucking say?' And all this. And I'm like, 'Ah lads, I was only . . . ' And then, one of them . . . he just gave me this unbelievable kick in the arse, you know? And it was so . . . it was so . . . the humiliation of it, like, and I . . .

RICHARD. Ah, Sharky . . .

SHARKY. I turned around and I threw a dig and I was . . . but there was loads of them and I got an awful couple of smacks in the . . . my nose was pumping, it's alright now, but I had to leg it back into the Elphin. The fucking . . . streams of toilet roll I had stuck up my nose . . . it was so . . . The Wolfes put me in a cab, gave your man twenty euros to drop me up.

Short pause.

RICHARD. Why didn't you say anything? (*Short pause.*) You fucking eejit!

SHARKY. Yeah, well, I'll get the toast.

SHARKY goes into the kitchen.

IVAN. Mmm . . .

RICHARD. I mean, what can you do with a fella like that?

IVAN. Yeah, it was . . . they were all . . . Nicky Giblin was telling me . . .

RICHARD. Yeah, well Nicky means well, I'm sure . . .

Short pause. IVAN *checks to see if* SHARKY *is in earshot.*

IVAN. Does Sharky know that Eileen is with Nicky now?

RICHARD. What? Ah, yeah . . . no that's . . . Sure that's . . . she called into me here about two weeks ago, did I tell you that?

IVAN. Who, Eileen?

RICHARD. Yeah, she was here, she does a morning or two cleaning for the Franciscan monks up there in the Friary. She called in to see if I was . . . to see how I was. We had smoked cod and chips from the chipper and everything. Ah, it was great, we were talking about Head-the-ball (*Sharky*) . . . and Nicky and . . . yeah, the whole . . .

IVAN. Ah I'm kind of avoiding Nicky, to be honest with you, Dick.

RICHARD. Why?

IVAN. Ah, there's just always some fucking shite going on and I'm . . .

IVAN *clams up as* SHARKY *returns with some toast.*

SHARKY. Can you see there, Ivan?

IVAN. I can just about . . .

SHARKY. Would you . . . ? (*Unsaid: 'help Richard'.*)

IVAN. Yeah, yeah, do you want some toast there, Dick?

IVAN *starts to very shakily butter some toast as* SHARKY *nips back into the kitchen to get some for himself.*

RICHARD. I tell you what I'd love. I'd love a big Irish breakfast! A big fry with all white pudding and a runny egg and all . . .

SHARKY *returns with his own toast and a carton of orange juice.*

Do you hear me, Sharky?

SHARKY. What?

RICHARD. We should be having a nice Christmassy breakfast. We have to get some decent grub in for tomorrow, Sharky, Christmas pud and the works. This is disgraceful!

SHARKY. Yeah, I'm going up now when I get dressed . . .

RICHARD. How will you go?

SHARKY. Do you have your car with you, Ivan?

Pause. IVAN *looks at him blankly.*

RICHARD. Do you have your car, Ivan?

IVAN. I can't . . . I don't know.

RICHARD. We'll go in a taxi.

SHARKY. Are you coming as well?

RICHARD. Ah, let me get out for a bit, for Jaysus' sake, Sharky, we might even get a Christmas pint . . .

SHARKY (*sighing*). Oh . . . well, wait now because if . . .

RICHARD. No, because we need to get a few bits in as well, Sharky, from the off-licence, in case anyone calls. We'll get

a taxi back, because I want to be settled in here now for
Christmas Eve . . .

SHARKY. Yeah, but wait a minute, because if I have to . . .

RICHARD (*suddenly despairing*). I have so little left to live
for!

Pause.

IVAN (*reassuringly*). Ah now, Richard . . .

RICHARD. What?! Yous don't know. Yous don't know.

SHARKY. No we'll all . . . we'll all go . . . we'll get the few
bits and . . .

IVAN. Sure you'll be grand, you'll have a grand Christmas
here with Sharky here, and with you and all, and . . .

RICHARD (*dismally*). Yeah . . .

SHARKY. If we're going out . . . will you have a wash?

RICHARD (*shouting*). I'll have a wash tomorrow!! I told you!
Now leave it!

Pause.

IVAN. God, I'll have to find my glasses. Karen'll kill me, God,
what am I gonna say?

SHARKY. We'll find them, I'll have a look now in a minute
before we go.

IVAN. Thanks, Sharky.

SHARKY. Tea, Rich?

RICHARD (*sheepishly*). Yeah, thanks.

SHARKY *brings him a cup of tea.*

I just don't want to be cooped up all over the . . .

SHARKY. Yeah, I know, we'll get out, we'll get you some
fresh air.

RICHARD. Yeah . . .

IVAN. Hey, any sign of your money there yet, Sharky? From the bus people?

SHARKY. What? Aw . . . Well, the . . .

RICHARD. Get this!

SHARKY. Well, no, because the solicitor fucking . . . he misdated the statement I gave him. About the . . . the actual night I fell down the stairs . . .

IVAN. What, the bus went round the wrong corner, or a different corner or something, was it?

SHARKY. Yeah, he went around the wrong corner up there at Christchurch there, he went around too early, and I was getting up to get off . . . but that's . . . no one is disputing that, but the date, you see, on the . . . affidavit, it's the wrong date and . . .

IVAN. Can you not just . . . ?

SHARKY. Nah, the courts are . . .

RICHARD. He put the wrong year on it!

SHARKY. The whole thing has been put right back now, I don't even know if . . .

IVAN. But can he not just change the . . .

RICHARD. It's a shambles . . .

IVAN. . . . the year . . .

SHARKY. No . . .

IVAN. . . . if it was just a mistake . . .

RICHARD. Ivan, the law . . . the law is the law. It has to be.

IVAN. Yeah . . .

SHARKY. So now I have to look at . . .

IVAN. Yeah, if you keep going with it . . .

SHARKY. No, if I want to start the whole thing off again . . .

IVAN. What?

RICHARD. Yeah. Seven-and-a-half years he's been . . .

SHARKY. Ah, it doesn't matter, it's too . . .

IVAN. Jaysus, that's a pain in the bollocks, isn't it?

SHARKY. Ah it's . . .

Waving it away.

IVAN. 'Cause I'd say you could've done with the few bob . . .

SHARKY. Yeah well . . .

IVAN. Nightmare . . .

RICHARD. Of course, he was using your man, that solicitor out of Kilbarrack.

SHARKY. Yeah, alright, Rich . . .

IVAN. That drinks in *The Fox & Hound*?!

RICHARD. Yeah, your man that does be falling around the car park!

SHARKY. Ah no, see it was him that . . .

RICHARD (*shaking his head*). Sharky . . .

SHARKY. I was never even gonna take a case! It was him that . . . I mean . . .

RICHARD. What a shambles . . .

SHARKY. Yeah, well . . .

IVAN. Aw well, I'm sorry to hear that, Shark. I only saw your man the other week there actually, and the Baker, and Steady Eddie and all them lads were down in Graingers, do you know what they were talking about? Do you remember Maurice Macken?

RICHARD. That used drive the milk lorry?

IVAN. Yeah, and then he got into the electrical trade. Do you remember him, Sharky?

SHARKY. The skinny fella?

IVAN. Yeah, Maurice Macken used play a lot of cards all up around Sutton and Howth, you heard what happened him?

RICHARD. Oh yeah, I heard all about that.

SHARKY. Was this in the paper?

IVAN. Yeah it was all in the paper, you would've seen it. He was electrocuted up in a house where he was working in Santry. There was a tremendous bang! Blew him right across the room, I believe. One of his fillings ended up in his ear. Somehow he survived. They let him go home out of Beaumont Hospital, and then there was a fire in his house that night! And he was gone!

RICHARD. Gobshite . . .

SHARKY. Jaysus, that's mad.

IVAN. His number was up! His number was just up and he was going to have to go, one way or the other, you know what I mean, mad! Survived the electrocution only to be burned!

RICHARD. Fucking eejit . . .

IVAN. But listen, what the lads were saying up in Grainger's – two people, two different people, now, have seen him hanging around at the off-licence serving hatch round the side near the car park.

RICHARD (*incredulously*). Come on!

IVAN. Two different people saw him, Dick, on different nights. And apparently a barman tidying up after they were closed said he heard someone shouting in the jacks – and when he went in, there was no one there.

RICHARD. That's bollocks.

IVAN. Yeah, well, apparently he looks really white. He was standing near the hatch. Big Bernard's cousin saw him. Apparently he was just standing there looking out into the car park, like he was waiting on a lift or something.

RICHARD. Go on out of that! What's he waiting on? A few cans?

He laughs.

IVAN (*to* SHARKY). Spooky though, isn't it?

SHARKY. Yeah, well . . .

RICHARD (*mildly derisive*). Yeah, right . . .

Suddenly there are three loud bangs at the front door upstairs. RICHARD *jumps with fright.*

Fucking hell! Who's that?

SHARKY (*going up the stairs*). Probably the postman . . .

RICHARD. We have a letterbox! For the love of God . . .

Short pause.

IVAN (*sighing*). Yeah . . .

RICHARD. Ivan, quick, where did he put that Gold Label?

IVAN (*quickly squinting around*). I can't fucking see, Dick . . .

RICHARD. Have a look in the kitchen, go on, quick.

IVAN *strides purposefully towards the kitchen.*

On top of the fridge or in the press with the pots . . .

IVAN *disappears into the kitchen and returns quickly with the bottle* SHARKY *put away earlier, unscrewing the lid . . .*

IVAN. Here, Rich, give us your cup.

RICHARD (*offering his cup of tea to* IVAN). Pour that out.

IVAN *takes* RICHARD*'s cup and wildly looks for somewhere to pour it out, deciding eventually to pour it on to the carpet nearby, bending low so as not to make a splashing sound, he then rubs the steaming carpet with his foot and pours a big dollop of whiskey into* RICHARD*'s cup, handing it to him.* RICHARD *raises it to his mouth immediately.* IVAN *goes to the table to look for a cup for himself, swigging a mouthful of whiskey from the neck of the bottle as he does so.*

He grabs a mug and pours some whiskey, wheeling around to give RICHARD *another shot, as* RICHARD *instinctively holds his cup out for it. Both men are retching and making faces as though their throats are burning. Their arms and legs undergo a rudimentary stretch as they seem to come alive. IVAN pours some tea on top of the whiskey in his cup and conceals the bottle while SHARKY appears at the top of the stairs, descending with a tastefully gift-wrapped box.*

(*Brightly.*) What was it, Shark?

SHARKY. Postman.

IVAN. Look at that!

RICHARD. What is it?

SHARKY. It's a . . . it's a present . . .

RICHARD. For who?

SHARKY. For me.

RICHARD. Who's it from?

SHARKY. Ah, the, the people I was working for down in Clare . . . His wife, Miriam, she's very . . . you know . . . (*To* IVAN.) She's a very nice lady, she's eh . . .

RICHARD. Wooooooooo! (*Childishly.*) The big birthday present!

SHARKY. It's a Christmas present, you dozy fucking eejit.

RICHARD. Oh! (*Same tone.*) A Christmas present! Anything good?

SHARKY (*handing* RICHARD *an envelope*). Here, there's a card here for you.

RICHARD. Who's it from?

SHARKY. The Department of Social Welfare.

RICHARD (*throwing it away*). Ah, that's only my balls!

SHARKY opens the card that came with his present and stands there reading it. IVAN slurps his tea . . .

Well? What is it?

SHARKY looks at him as though coming out of a daze . . .

SHARKY. What?

IVAN. Are you gonna open it up?

RICHARD. Yes! Cheer us all up! Presents arriving for Sharky!
I mean, what next?

SHARKY *takes the wrapping off . . .*

What is it?

SHARKY. It's a few CDs.

IVAN. Nice one!

RICHARD (*childishly*). Wooooooo, music to put you in the
mood . . . ! For getting in your nude . . . !

IVAN. Hey, she knows her stuff! Some of these are classics!
Here, put one on!

RICHARD. No! Later! We have to go and get the few bits for
the Christmas! Come on . . .

IVAN. I have to find my glasses!

RICHARD. Sharky'll look for them. Sharky, have a quick look
for Ivan's specs, will you?

SHARKY. Where would they be, Ivan? Where did you sleep?

IVAN. Eh, in the box room.

SHARKY. There's no bed in there!

IVAN. I slept on the rug.

SHARKY. The rug?

RICHARD. Ah, Ivan . . .

IVAN. Ah, no, there was towels, and there was . . .

SHARKY. I'll have a quick look. (*Going off up the stairs.*) You
should've slept in the spare room . . .

IVAN. Ah no, I was grand I was fine . . .

RICHARD. Did you just sleep on the floor? Like an animal?

IVAN. No, I slept on the rug.

RICHARD. Ah, I don't even know what you're talking about. Give us a hand, Ivan, will you?

IVAN (*helping* RICHARD *up*). I thought Sharky was in the spare room.

RICHARD. I often just go off here at the fire. (*He coughs up some deeply embedded old phlegm and rubs it into the side of his armchair.*) You should have got into my bed.

IVAN. Nah, I wouldn't do that, Dick. Here, do you want your shoes?

RICHARD. Ah, sure we'll get a taxi, my slippers is grand. I don't expect we'll be walking the street like hobos. Just get us my anorak hanging up there behind the kitchen door.

IVAN *goes to the kitchen.* RICHARD *feels around for his cup.* IVAN *brings the anorak and starts looking for his own coat.*

Is that Gold Label dead? We have to make a list. We have nothing organised. That's your man, of course. He was supposed to get up to me weeks ago. His head is arseways. You're seeing him on the dry now, that's why he's running around in here like a fly in a bottle.

IVAN *finds his own coat which he puts on and goes to retrieve the bottle from whatever nook he hid it in. There is only a swig left in it.*

But of course then with jar on him he's worse! Throwing digs outside the Elphin! Or getting in mills outside the chipper on Kilbarrack Road the last time he was here! Getting arrested by the Guards up in Howth! I mean what am I going to do?

As IVAN *drains the last shot of whiskey straight from the bottle . . .*

Here, is there a shot left in that Powers, Ivan?

IVAN. Nah, we've had it. Here do you want your anorak, Dick?

RICHARD (*sighing heavily*). Yeah . . .

IVAN *helps* RICHARD *to put his coat on.*

Here, if you're gonna be round tomorrow, you should drop
in, do you know what I have that I've been saving? A drop
of Brigid Blake's poteen, that Big Bernard got me . . .

IVAN. Oh, look out!

RICHARD. That'll fucking . . .

He makes a high-pitched whistle, pointing to his head.
IVAN *laughs.* SHARKY *descends. He has got dressed and
wears his coat.*

SHARKY. Ivan, I can't see your glasses anywhere.

RICHARD. Ah they have to be somewhere, Sharky!

SHARKY. Do you not have a spare pair at home'll do you
till . . . ?

IVAN. Yeah, I think I . . . they're an older prescription, if I can
find them . . . Oh God, Karen is gonna kill me.

RICHARD. No, no she won't! I'll ring her, I'll say I had them
here, it'll be grand. Sharky, get a pen, we need to make a
list. Ivan I expect we'll be seeing you over the Christmas,
I'll be very disappointed if we didn't, so Sharky, Harp,
what, four six packs?

SHARKY (*grabbing a pen*). Yeah, Harp . . .

IVAN. Ah, don't just do that for me, Rich. Sharky, I'll drink
whatever's going.

RICHARD (*pointing imperiously*). No. Sharky.

SHARKY (*writing*). Yeah, Harp. Stout, Richard?

RICHARD. Yeah and Paddy Powers. Get three bottles.

SHARKY. Three bottles? The off-licence is open again on
Monday, Rich.

RICHARD. If we have visitors they may want a hot whiskey.
It's called being festive. I know you may not comprehend it,
Sharky, but some us like to be social. Ivan, Christmas? You
have to!

IVAN. Ah, Christmas is great!

RICHARD. And Miller for Nicky.

SHARKY. For Nicky Giblin?

RICHARD. Nicky drinks Miller, Sharky. We all understand that you have issues with life and it's an endless struggle for you to grasp human relationships, but Nicky is a friend of mine. And a friend of Ivan's . . . and . . .

IVAN. Ah., he can be very messy, Richard.

RICHARD (*with finality*). The man is welcome here!

SHARKY (*writing*). Bottles of Miller.

RICHARD. Thank you.

SHARKY. What'll I get for tomorrow? A chicken?

RICHARD. Turkey! Turkey!

SHARKY. We won't get a turkey now at this stage, Rich . . .

IVAN. Karen is doing us a big turkey tomorrow, I could drop down with maybe a few . . .

RICHARD. No, no, Ivan we couldn't do that to you, we'll get a turkey, don't worry about it . . .

SHARKY (*sucking his pen*). I mean we might be able to get a piece of em . . .

RICHARD. Look! Let's go!

SHARKY. Do you not want to make a list?

RICHARD. Yeah, yeah, we'll get all that when we're there. We'll see all that. Ivan will you take me out the back way and we'll hail a taxi on the road, I want to check them awful fucking winos haven't been messing around at our laneway door.

IVAN *is leading* RICHARD *out towards the yard.*

Will you lock up, Sharky?

SHARKY. Yeah.

RICHARD. We'll see you out on the road. (*As they go.*) All the kids' presents got then, Ivan?

IVAN. Ah, yeah . . . I think they are.

RICHARD. Well, I hope so, says you!

As they leave through the back door, SHARKY *folds up the list and puts it in his pocket. He takes out his keys and goes to lock the back door. He comes back into the silence and picks up the card he received. He looks at it for a moment, then briskly puts it in his pocket and leaves, running up the stairs.*

We hear the wind and perhaps music plays as the lights slowly change from bright morning to a dusky feel and we slide into:

Scene Two

The wind is picking up outside as the sunlight fades and the temperature drops. The music dies away as SHARKY *comes down the stairs with bags of shopping, mostly from the off-licence, which he takes into the kitchen. A church bell chimes solemnly somewhere off in the distance. He reappears, switches on a lamp or two, bends down under the scraggy old Christmas tree and plugs in some coloured fairy lights. He sees two little presents wrapped up there. He picks one up and looks at it for a moment, wondering about it before he puts it back. He goes back up the stairs, pausing to tap the extinguished light under the Sacred Heart. It doesn't come on and he continues up to the hall to get the rest of the shopping and reappears, carrying more bags. As he descends we hear* RICHARD *calling from off, up in the hallway.*

RICHARD (*off*). What are you fucking doing?

SHARKY (*halting and turning*). What?

RICHARD (*off*). What, were you gonna just leave me up here?

SHARKY. I thought you could manage your way down!

RICHARD (*off*). Ah, not when I'm jarred, Sharky!

SHARKY. Just give me a second.

SHARKY *carries the bags down, leaving them at the bottom of the stairs, and makes his way back up.*

RICHARD (*off*). I'm freezing!

SHARKY *reappears, helping* RICHARD *down.*

You are in one foul humour today . . .

SHARKY. Richard, now, please don't start . . .

RICHARD (*warmly, paternally*). What's the matter with you?

SHARKY. Richard . . .

RICHARD. What . . .

SHARKY. Nothing's the matter with me.

RICHARD *stands in the room rubbing his hands.* SHARKY *starts clearing a few things away, taking the breakfast things on a tray into the kitchen.*

RICHARD. God, it's freezing! Would you get the fire going for the love of Jaysus, Shark?

SHARKY. I am! I'm doing it! I've a million things to do here, just give me a second, would you?

RICHARD (*as though* SHARKY *has completely overreacted*). Okay! Okay!

SHARKY *returns, goes to the stove, puts some peat briquettes in and sets about lighting it.*

God, I never seen such a Christmas wrecker! Would you not have left the old Kaliber out for today and had a drink with me and Ivan . . . and . . .

SHARKY (*working at the stove*). I'm pissed *off* with you, Richard.

RICHARD. With me? Why? What did I do now?

SHARKY. What did you have to go and invite Nicky Giblin up here for?

RICHARD. When?

SHARKY. When Big Bernard let you speak to him on his
mobile.

RICHARD. Ah that was only a Happy Christmas, Jimmy,
come on . . .

SHARKY. You told him to call in to us . . .

RICHARD. But sure, that's what you say! That's what
everybody says!

SHARKY. You told him to call in to play cards!

RICHARD. That's . . . that's just what you say! Anyway – so
what?! Would you stop being such a curmudgeonly old
bollocks your whole life, will you?

Pause. SHARKY *works . . .*

(*Warmly, drunkenly conciliatory.*) Ah, Sharky . . . I only
said to stick the head in if he was in the area . . .

SHARKY. You don't fucking say that to fellas like Nicky,
Dick. He'll be in on top of us before you know it!

RICHARD. No he won't! He was elephants! He was down in
the Brookwood Inn of all places! How the hell is he gonna
rock up here? In a taxi? I don't think so! Hey, is there 'ere a
Christmas drink going a-begging around here?

SHARKY. Yeah, well I saw him the other day, and he was
driving my car, Richard.

RICHARD. Who?

SHARKY. Nicky Giblin!

RICHARD. Yeah, well you gave your car to Eileen!

SHARKY. I loaned it to her for the school run, Dick. I didn't
ever expect to see that fucker driving around in it! I saw
him pulling out of the shops down there in Bayside, and I
was walking down to get the Dart in the pissing rain! And
he was in my car!

RICHARD. Ah, grow up, Sharky! What do you want? Him and
Eileen are together now, so get over it, 'cause that's life,
okay? Now would you ever give us a Jaysus fucking drink,
you're gonna blow the whole Christmas atmosphere. This is
all I have! And how many do I have left? Maybe only this
one! Maybe that's it for me!

SHARKY. What are you talking about?

RICHARD. Ah! It's hardly even worth it! . . . What's the point?

RICHARD *turns away in disgust.* SHARKY *takes the rest of
the shopping into the kitchen.* RICHARD *opens his coat
and makes his way unsteadily towards his armchair and sits
forlornly.* SHARKY *re-emerges with a glass of whiskey for
him.*

SHARKY. Here . . . Richard . . .

RICHARD. What?

SHARKY (*putting the drink in* RICHARD's *hand*). Here . . .

RICHARD. Ah, thanks, Sharky.

SHARKY *takes a festive-looking candle in a red glass
holder from a bag. He is tearing the price and the cellophane
wrapping off and bringing it to the window sill.*

What's that?

SHARKY. Hmm?

RICHARD. What are you doing, there?

SHARKY. Ah, I'm just gonna put an old candle in the window.

RICHARD. Ah, that's nice. That's more like it, Sharky. I never
like it when you're down. It changes the whole . . .

SHARKY. Would you like some smoked salmon and brown
bread?

RICHARD. Oh, now, that sounds . . . Ah, thanks, Sharky . . .
thanks. Delicious!

SHARKY. Keep us going anyway . . . Is that getting warm?

RICHARD. Oh, we're warming up now . . .

SHARKY *goes towards the kitchen.*

Oh, Sharky. Just one . . . just one small thing, quickly,
before you do that.

SHARKY. Yeah?

RICHARD. You wouldn't take a basin of hot water down out
to the back door at the lane . . . ? Them filthy fucking winos
have all puke and piss and everything else all down our step
all up the fucking door out there . . .

SHARKY *(face dropping)*. Are you serious?

RICHARD. Ah, it's absolutely disgusting. We can't leave it like
that on Christmas Eve . . . It'll only take you a minute . . .
Good man . . .

SHARKY *goes unhappily to the kitchen to boil the kettle.*
RICHARD *cosily raises his shoulders as though he is
snuggling down into a lovely warm bed.*

Now, this is nice now. It's getting nice and Christmassy
now . . .

There is a loud rapping at the front door upstairs. RICHARD
turns to profile. SHARKY *steps back into the room . . .*

Sharky!

SHARKY. I hear it.

RICHARD. Well, get it, will you!

SHARKY. I'm not gonna get it, I told you I don't want Nicky
Giblin in here, I just don't want it.

RICHARD. What!?

There are more loud raps at the door . . .

SHARKY. I told you, Richard! Why do you have to do this to
me?

RICHARD. What are you talking about? I'm not doing
anything to you. Don't be a fucking child, will you, and get
the door, for God's sake . . .

SHARKY just stands there looking at RICHARD.
RICHARD suddenly bursts up out of his chair . . .

I'll get it myself!

With surprising speed, RICHARD darts towards the staircase.
He hits the wall, collapses, bounces up again, grabs the
banister and attempts to pull himself up the stairs . . .

SHARKY. Richard! Hold on, will you?

SHARKY runs across and grabs RICHARD. RICHARD
stumbles and falls backwards into SHARKY's arms, the
two of them sinking to the ground as the doorbell rings.

RICHARD. What are you fucking doing?!

SHARKY. What are you fucking doing? Come back over here
and sit down, will you?

SHARKY bundles RICHARD towards his chair . . .

For fuck's sake . . .

RICHARD. Will you get the door?

SHARKY. Yeah, will you just sit down please?

SHARKY storms angrily off up the stairs. RICHARD gets
up and feels around for his glass which has fallen
somewhere . . . We hear SHARKY's voice off upstairs . . .

(*Off.*) No, no, it's no problem! Don't be silly . . . come on,
come on down to Richard.

IVAN (*off*). I'm sorry, Sharky.

SHARKY leads IVAN down.

I'm sorry, Richard, I'm sorry to . . .

RICHARD. Who is it? Ivan?

IVAN. Richard, I'm sorry, I'm barging in on you again . . . I'm
sorry, Sharky . . .

SHARKY. No . . .

RICHARD. What's the matter with you?

IVAN. Karen's after completely doing her nut.

RICHARD. What? Why?

IVAN. Ah, even if I . . . I should've just gone straight home
it might have been different. But after you left and I was
gonna head, I was just standing outside Doyle's with Big
Bernard having a smoke, she was coming out of the post
office and I didn't have my glasses and I didn't see her
and . . .

RICHARD. Did you not get your spare glasses?

IVAN. I didn't even get in the house, Dick! She fucking reefed
me out of it! (*His face crumples in pain.*) The kids were
there and . . . (*A sudden impassioned plea.*) I only went in
to have that quick one with yous! I was on my way home!
Yous know that! But sure then there was people buying me
Christmas pints left and right – I couldn't even see who they
were to say to say no! (*He sinks into a chair.*) This is a
disaster!

RICHARD. Ah now, come on, Ivan . . .

IVAN. I hate it when the kids see us fighting and . . .

RICHARD. These things happen.

IVAN. Now I'm after ruining Christmas on them all (*Beat.*)
again!

RICHARD. No, you haven't! She'll calm down . . . Just take it
easy . . . Sharky, where's your manners? Will you get poor
Ivan something to drink?

SHARKY. I'll tell you what. I've a nice bit of smoked salmon
we were gonna have, and there's little mince pies I was
gonna heat up. Will you have one, Ivan?

IVAN (*rubbing his face*). Oh, I don't know . . .

SHARKY. Ah, it'll do you good, Ivan . . .

IVAN. I suppose . . . thanks, Sharky.

RICHARD. Yeah, great, and get him a drink, will you, Sharky?
Good man.

SHARKY *goes to the kitchen.*

Now, not to worry, Ivan. The woman is being completely unreasonable, she'll come round, just you watch. And we'll be nice and cosy here now and we'll figure it out . . .

SHARKY *returns with some glasses, a can of Harp for* IVAN, *and a bottle of whiskey for* RICHARD.

Sharky. (*A little laugh.*) Excuse me, I lost my drink in the . . . in the confusion there . . .

SHARKY. I have one here for you.

RICHARD. Ah, thanks. Hey, I know! Sharky'll go back up with you, Ivan.

SHARKY *impotently shoots a look at* RICHARD.

Sharky, you'll explain! His glasses have to be here somewhere! And we can . . .

IVAN. Oh, I don't know, I wouldn't go up there now at the moment, Sharky. She absolutely now . . . she fucking reefed me out of it. There was people all standing there looking at us . . . even Bernard just went back in. It was awful. The kids were there . . .

RICHARD. No, no, we'll let her cool down, absolutely . . .

SHARKY *gives* IVAN *a glass of beer.*

IVAN. Thanks, Sharky.

RICHARD. Yeah, and get the mince pies, we'll get nice and Christmassy here now.

SHARKY. Yeah, I've the oven heating up.

RICHARD. Oh and listen, don't forget to wash that auld step and the door in the lane, will you?

SHARKY. Yeah, I'll do it . . .

RICHARD. Good man, Sharky.

SHARKY *goes.*

(*Raising his glass, brightly.*) Now! Happy Christmas!

IVAN. Yeah . . . happy Christmas . . .

RICHARD. Sure here we are, aren't we? Ha? We're having a nice Christmas drink. And we'll let the whole . . . Ivan, are you listening to me?

IVAN. Yeah. No, I am . . .

RICHARD. The whole situation will . . . (*He signals 'Settle down'.*) And we'll talk to her and . . . And we'll all be right as dodgers. Do you hear me?

IVAN. Yeah, I'm sorry, Richard.

RICHARD. No, no, no, no, no, no, no . . . Come on! When I used clean windows all up along, all up the coast all up into Sutton, I saw every conceivable kind of men and women all shacked up in myriad . . . (*With sudden force.*) myriad, states of confusion and banjaxed relationships. Believe me, she'd have been rid of you long ago at this stage if your marriage wasn't strong enough to weather a tiny little bump every now and again . . . (*He laughs.*) It's Christmas Eve! Ivan. Ivan . . .

IVAN just looks up silently into RICHARD's blind eyes. The doorbell rings, a loud cutting sound. IVAN looks up and then back at RICHARD. Pause.

(*Calling.*) SHARKY! (*Pause.*) Ah he's out the back. You wouldn't go up and answer that for us, would you, Ivan?

IVAN. Yeah, no . . .

He shoots his drink back and goes up the stairs.

RICHARD. Ah thanks, good man. (*Starts to sing tunelessly.*) 'Oh the weather outside is frightening, it's dark and there's thunder and lightning . . .'

He suddenly hunches and shudders, holding his shoulders as though someone has walked over his grave. We hear voices off and then see NICKY's legs descending. It is completely dark outside by now.

NICKY (*off*). Oh yeah, yeah, yeah, yeah, yeah, yeah, no, yeah! (*In Irish.*) 'Is mise le meas, Sean Lemass!' (*He laughs.*) Did you see all the Christmas lights all up the . . . Aw no, no, no, no, no, no . . . We won't stay long if he's . . . Come down Mr Lockhart!

NICKY descends into the room followed by IVAN and LOCKHART.

RICHARD (*rising*). Nicky!

NICKY. Happy Christmas! Happy Christmas! Happy Christmas!

NICKY GIBLIN has a skinny, nervy appearance. He rarely seems in bad humour. He is about SHARKY's age or maybe younger. He wears a tatty-looking anorak and threadbare grey slacks that are slightly too short for him, revealing white towelling sport socks in low-cut, dark, wine-coloured slip-on shoes. LOCKHART is a man in his fifties perhaps. He is well-dressed with a camel hair Crombie overcoat, a silk scarf, a fine trilby hat and an expensive-looking suit. He looks like a wealthy businessman and bon viveur. Both he and NICKY glow warmly with festive indulgence.

RICHARD. And a Happy Christmas to you, Nicky!

They embrace fondly. NICKY produces a gift-wrapped bottle of whiskey from his anorak pocket.

NICKY. And I brought you just a little . . .

RICHARD (*mildly remonstrating*). Ah, Nicky . . .

NICKY (*dismissive*). Ah, go on, would you? Sure where you would you be without the old Christmas, and I was just saying to . . . Sorry, this is . . . Richard this is Mr Lockhart.

RICHARD. Mr Lockhart! Pleased to meet you. Seasons' greetings!

LOCKHART. And to you too, Mr Harkin. I hope you don't mind us crashing in on you here now . . .

RICHARD. What are you talking about? Not at all! Not at all! Of course not! Will you have a drop of . . . Nicky! We have Miller! Ivan, will you get a glass there for . . . I got Miller

in especially for you, Nicky. Ivan, it's in the . . . it's
probably in the kitchen there. Ask Sharky, will you?

NICKY. Is Sharky here?

RICHARD. Mr Lockhart? Will you have a drop? Is this what
I think it is? Or a drop of stout or . . .

LOCKHART. I'll take a small Irish whiskey if you have it, Mr
Harkin.

NICKY. And you do have it! Right there!

RICHARD. Ah, Nicky . . . And Mr Lockhart, please, call me
Richard . . . Ivan, here will you . . .

He holds the bottle out.

IVAN. Ha?

RICHARD. Will you take this and . . . (*Thinks better of it.*)
or actually, just bring me a glass for Mr Lockhart, and a
bottle of Miller for Nicky out of the fridge there, or it
should be . . . just ask Sharky. Please excuse me, Mr
Lockhart. Unfortunately my sight is . . . I fell into a skip
and I . . .

I have no sight.

IVAN goes to the kitchen.

LOCKHART. God help you.

RICHARD. And this is my, this is my first Christmas here in
the dark, so to speak . . . so it's eh . . .

LOCKHART. Yes. But let me say, you have a fine holy glow
off you, all the same.

RICHARD. I say me prayers!

LOCKHART. I can see it.

NICKY. And the old mind burns brightly, Richard, ha?

RICHARD. Ah, well, I don't know . . .

NICKY. No, no! To me, here now, sure you seem absolutely no
different at all.

RICHARD. Ah, Nicky . . .

NICKY. No, it's true! So you got out for a Christmas drink?

RICHARD. Yes! We were down in Doyle's. Ivan was there and Big Bernard and Steady Eddie and the bouncy castle fella was singing hymns and, ah, it was brilliant . . .

IVAN returns with a drink for NICKY, a glass for LOCKHART and a glass for himself. The glasses are somewhat mixed and unsuitable but usable, e.g. perhaps he is using a little jug for himself . . .

NICKY (*to* IVAN). Is Sharky here?

IVAN. I think he's out in the . . .

RICHARD. Ah, don't mind him, he's off the drink – for Christmas! – and he has all our heads wrecked. So tell us, where were you? (*Proffering bottle.*) Here, Mr Lockhart!

NICKY takes the bottle from RICHARD to pour a drink for LOCKHART.

NICKY. Where weren't we? Is the question! Good God – we've been . . . Well, what happened was, I'd a few bits to do with Eileen down in Killester, so she went off and I went into the Beachcomber – fucking nobody in it! (*To* LOCKHART.) What time was that at?

LOCKHART. About twelve?

NICKY. Twelve o'clock, nobody in there. I think, 'Right, I'll just have a quick pint and head on . . . ' But then I see Mr Lockhart is sitting up at the bar, who I know from up in the Marine . . . Mr Lockhart, you'd do a lot of your drinking up in the Marine Hotel . . .

LOCKHART. I've been known to frequent the premises . . .

They all laugh.

NICKY. And we know each other from me calling up there to see my brother Eric . . . so we have a pint, but there was no atmosphere, so fuck it, we left – up to the Yacht.

LOCKHART. No, Harry Byrne's.

NICKY. Sorry no, Harry Byrne's . . .

RICHARD. Oh, very posh!

NICKY (*pouring drinks for* LOCKHART, RICHARD *and* IVAN). Oh yeah, they had the fires lit and then we were in the Yacht . . . which was hopping.

RICHARD. Jaysus, yous were getting around!

NICKY. That was only the start of it! The Yacht, the Dollymount House . . .

LOCKHART. The Raheny Inn . . .

NICKY. The Raheny Inn, the Green Dolphin, the Station House, the Cedars, the Elphin – your man (*indicating* LOCKHART) won't let me put my hand in my pocket – this is taxis everywhere now!

RICHARD. Very wise . . . God yous were . . .

NICKY. Then back all the way up to Edenmore, Eugene's, the Concorde . . . the bleeding Brookwood Inn! (*He laughs.*) And then up here.

RICHARD. My God, that's a right Christmas drink, Nicky!

NICKY. Yeah well, Mr Lockhart had to say happy Christmas to a few people . . . (*Suddenly to* LOCKHART.) We never tracked them down!

LOCKHART. And I'm glad we didn't! Because we would never have made it up here! Anyway, as soon as a sing-along starts, I'm out of a place, that's just the way I am . . . But we're here now, and that's it!

RICHARD. Well, I'm glad you're here!

LOCKHART. Yes, and we'll say Happy Christmas – (*He raises his glass in a toast.*) and we'll have a toast . . .

NICKY (*raising glass*). Yes.

IVAN *has just taken a big gulp of whiskey. His glass is empty, so he spits the whiskey back into the glass for the toast . . .*

LOCKHART. To old friends and old times!

RICHARD. And new friends!

NICKY. Exactly! Cheers!

RICHARD. Happy Christmas!

NICKY. Happy Christmas!

They all drink deeply.

(*Taking the bottle to give refills.*) So where's Sharky? God, I haven't seen him in ages . . .

RICHARD. Ivan, get Sharky there, will you?

IVAN. Yeah, I'll . . .

He goes out through the kitchen.

RICHARD. There's a good man.

NICKY. How is he doing? Alright?

RICHARD. Ah, Nicky, sure you know yourself. This is my brother, Mr Lockhart. He claims he's here to look after me, but between ourselves, he's an awful useless fucking eejit, God love him. I don't know who's looking after who!

NICKY. Sure you'd be well able to look after yourself, Dick . . .

RICHARD. This is it. If they can get me one of those dogs that bring you your meals . . . or even someone just to do a tiny bit of shopping. Sure all I really need is the bit of company really.

NICKY. Well, I knew you'd up for a bit of companionship and when I mentioned to Mr Lockhart that there might be an old game of cards on the horizon, he was very, eh . . .

LOCKHART. Well, there's nothing like a game of cards at Christmas.

RICHARD. You're so right! And you're welcome, Mr Lockhart. We're only amateurs now you understand.

NICKY. Go on out of that! You'll have to watch yourself, Mr Lockhart, you'll be fleeced for Christmas!

RICHARD. Yeah, right!

LOCKHART. No fear! I'm not a big gambler myself necessarily. To be honest with you I just like the social . . . ness and the crack.

RICHARD. Well, this is it! There's no big gamblers here, Mr Lockhart. Why can't a game of cards be just for fun? You know what I mean?

SHARKY and IVAN appear from the kitchen. SHARKY is wearing an apron and rubber gloves and carrying a filthy cloth. Pause.

NICKY. Ah, there you are, Sharky! Happy Christmas!

NICKY goes to him to shake hands. SHARKY removes a glove to shake his hand dutifully.

SHARKY. Yeah, happy Christmas, Nicky.

NICKY. Eileen sends her regards. We hope you'll pop in over the . . .

SHARKY. Yeah, sure . . .

NICKY. This is Mr Lockhart.

LOCKHART. Sharky. A pleasure.

SHARKY. How do you do.

As they shake hands, SHARKY is wondering where he knows LOCKHART from.

NICKY. Mr Lockhart said he'd pop in to help us make up the old numbers for a game of cards . . .

LOCKHART. I hope you don't mind, Sharky . . .

SHARKY. No. I just didn't know we were playing cards.

NICKY. Ah, it's a tradition, Sharky! Ivan, you'll play . . .

IVAN. Well, yeah, I'll . . . No, I've no . . . I've no money on me 'cause . . .

RICHARD. Don't worry about that, Ivan. Of course he'll play, we'll all play!

SHARKY (*to* RICHARD). How will you read your cards?

RICHARD. Ivan and me'll play together! Ivan, you can read our cards and I'll bankroll us. How does that sound?

IVAN. Yeah, that's . . . that'd suit me . . .

RICHARD. And we'll split our takings fifty-fifty. Sure, I'm probably gonna have to bankroll Sharky anyway!

NICKY. Ivan'll be the eyes and Richard'll be the ears!

RICHARD. And the brains!

LOCKHART. Now, you're sure I'm not barging in on your . . .

RICHARD. Not at all! Not at all! You're welcome. We'll take all of Nicky's money. Do you have any collateral, Nicky?

NICKY. Always. Feel that.

He holds out his arm for RICHARD.

RICHARD. Feel what?

NICKY. You feel that fabric?

RICHARD *feels the arm of* NICKY*'s anorak.*

RICHARD. Oh, nice!

NICKY. This is a Versace jacket.

RICHARD. Yes . . .

IVAN. Is it?

NICKY (*to* IVAN). Feel that.

RICHARD. It's nice . . .

NICKY. You feel that? It's dog's skin.

IVAN. What?

NICKY (*laughing*). No, it's not dog's skin. It's called dog's skin. It's German. Right, Mr Lockhart?

LOCKHART. Yup.

RICHARD. It's nice, Nicky.

IVAN (*incredulous*). That's a Versace jacket?

NICKY (*defensively*). Yeah . . . Well . . . no, like it needs a
    wash for Christmas, only 'cause I wear it all the time, but
    it's eh . . . yeah, you know?

RICHARD. You might tell Sharky where he'd get a nice jacket
    like that, Nicky.

NICKY. Jacket like this? Two, three grand, Richard.

IVAN. What?!

NICKY. Oh, big time! Oh here, Ivan, are you still driving that
    old orange Ford Fiesta?

IVAN. Yeah . . .

NICKY. 'Cause didn't we see, Mr Lockhart? There was a load
    of old winos out there sitting on it, you don't want that.

IVAN. What? Is my car here?

NICKY. Yeah. (*To* LOCKHART.) Didn't I point it out to you?
    And I fucking said it . . .

LOCKHART. Yeah, it's parked up around the other side of the
    green out there sort of half up on the path on the corner.

RICHARD (*springing into action*). Them fucking winos!!
    Come on, we can go out this way! Ivan, give me a hand.
    Show us where, Nicky.

SHARKY. Richard!

RICHARD *goes towards the kitchen, taking hold of* IVAN's
arm.

RICHARD. We won't be long, Mr Lockhart. The winos are
    always scared of me. Drinking that old meths always has
    them nervy, you see. Sharky, you look after Mr Lockhart.
    Come on! We'll have them gone out of it now, lickity spit.

NICKY. We're not gonna be getting in a fight, are we?

RICHARD. No, no, they'll run off immediately. We'll be back
    in a minute. Come on, Ivan! Nicky, hit that light out there
    for yourselves.

NICKY. Yeah, I got it.

NICKY *hits a switch as* IVAN *opens the back door and leads* RICHARD *out, followed by* NICKY. SHARKY *and* LOCKHART *are alone.* SHARKY *shakes his head at* LOCKHART.

LOCKHART. I know. Family, ha?

SHARKY. Yeah, don't talk to me. Are you okay for a drink there or . . .

LOCKHART. Yeah, I'm grand. You not having a drink yourself?

SHARKY. Nah . . . I'm . . . trying to . . . not drink.

LOCKHART. If you can just beat Christmas, ha?

SHARKY (*with a little laugh*). Yeah . . .

LOCKHART. If I can just beat Christmas I can achieve anything!

SHARKY. Mmm.

LOCKHART. But it's so hard. 'Cause the old drink stops the brain cranking. Stops the mind going into the forest.

SHARKY *is looking at* LOCKHART, *wondering about him.*

(*Knowingly.*) Oh yes, I've seen you on your travels. You don't remember me, Sharky . . .

SHARKY (*trying to place him*). No, I . . . I do . . .

LOCKHART. Yeah, I've seen you. On your wandering ways. I've seen you going down Wicklow Street, and halfway up Dame Street, down Suffolk Street, Grafton Street, Dawson Street, round and round, back up, back down, am I right? (*Pause.*) I've seen all those hopeless thoughts, buried there, in your stupid scrunched-up face.

SHARKY. What are you talking about?

LOCKHART. Oh, come on, Sharky! You don't remember me?

SHARKY. No, I . . . I do. But where did we . . . ?

LOCKHART. We met in the Bridewell, Sharky.

Short pause.

Remember? We were locked up in a cell together. You'd had a bit of bother the night before . . . ? You were waiting to go up before the judge in the morning . . . We played cards!

SHARKY. Yeah . . . no . . . I remember you, but . . .

LOCKHART (*brightly*). So how have things been with you?

SHARKY. . . . . Okay . . .

LOCKHART. Not great though . . .

Pause.

SHARKY. You've a good memory.

LOCKHART. Old as the hills, Sharky. You know I was sure I'd run into you today. (*Laughs.*) But you're off the drink! Now that completely threw me, I have to say! Do you know how many pubs I was in?

SHARKY. What, were you looking for me?

LOCKHART. Well, it's just that matter we discussed back then, in the Bridewell that night.

Short pause.

SHARKY. This has to be what? Twenty years ago!

LOCKHART. Twenty-five years ago. But I'm still surprised you don't know why I'm here.

SHARKY. Yeah, well I don't.

LOCKHART (*disappointed*). Ah, Sharky . . . We had a deal. (*Short pause.*) No?

SHARKY. Look, I don't know what's going on here, or if Nicky's put you up to this, but I have to say I don't know what you're talking about.

LOCKHART. Are you serious?

SHARKY. Do I look like I'm telling a joke?

LOCKHART. No, hold on. You're seriously standing there telling me that it's never struck you as odd, down all these years, that you just walked out of jail? After what you did? Ah, that's brilliant, Sharky!

SHARKY. What do you mean 'after what I did'?

LOCKHART. Oh, come on, now . . .

SHARKY. What? What did I . . . I can't even . . . What? I got into a fight with some wino in the back of a shebeen up in . . . Francis Street or . . . somewhere, was it? I can hardly even remember! So what?

LOCKHART. Well no, not quite. His name was Laurence Joyce. He was sixty-one. He was a vagrant. He said he was trying to get to Cardiff . . . ? Said he had some family there . . . ? Said his wife was once the Cardiff Rose? You beat him up in the back of O'Dowd's public house in the early hours of the twenty fourth of December 1981. You killed him. (*Short pause.*) I let you out. I set you free.

Pause.

SHARKY. No, here, wait a minute . . .

LOCKHART. Come on, you remember. Remember in the morning, that moment when the guards opened the door, and told you to get your stuff and get lost?

SHARKY. . . . Yeah?

LOCKHART. I organised that. Because you won that hand of poker we were playing.

SHARKY. Wait a minute. That fella didn't die!

LOCKHART. Oh no. He did. What, are you trying to tell me you don't see him in your nightmares?

Pause. SHARKY *doesn't respond.*

God, the poor old brain hasn't aged too well, has it, Sharky? Look at you. Twenty-five years on the lash like some old borderline wino yourself. What chance haven't you fucked up? Driving the van for those English fellas? Or when you blew that nice cushy security job on the building site in Naas? You make me laugh, Sharky. Tell me, are you still in the wars with Dublin Bus about the night you were pissed

and you fell down the stairs? How much are you looking
for? For that twinge in your back?

Pause. SHARKY *is staring at* LOCKHART, *dumbfounded.*

You even blew that chauffeur job down in Lahinch!
(*Darkly.*) You fancied your man's wife, didn't you?

SHARKY. Who are you?

LOCKHART. Ah, Sharky . . . don't say you don't know who
I am. (*Short pause.*) Or what I want.

SHARKY. Well, I don't know!

LOCKHART. You don't remember we played cards?

SHARKY. No, I kind of do but . . .

LOCKHART. Poor Sharky. It's always a bit hazy, isn't it?
(*Short pause.*) I want your soul, Sharky.

SHARKY. What?

LOCKHART. I want your soul.

SHARKY. What the hell are you talking about? Is this some
kind of stupid fucking joke of Nicky's?

LOCKHART *just looks at him.* SHARKY *seems to feel
queasy and then enters the grip of some greater pain. It's so
excruciating that he starts to sink pathetically to his knees.
He tries to get a grip on something but ends up on all fours
fighting the urge to pass out, so great is the agony – both
physically and deep within his mind.*

LOCKHART. I'm the son of the morning, Sharky. I'm the
snake in the garden. I've come here for your soul this
Christmas, and I've been looking for you all fucking day!
We made a deal. We played cards for your freedom and you
promised me, you promised me, the chance to play you
again. So don't start messing me about now. (*Short pause.*)
Of course, after you skipped merrily off to some early
house in the morning you probably never even thought
about it again, did you? Ha? You think I'm just farting
around? You think you're better than me? Pig. Well, think
again. Because we're gonna play for your soul and I'm

gonna win and you're coming through the old hole in the wall with me tonight. Now get up.

SHARKY *is silently crying as he staggers back to his feet.* LOCKHART *suddenly bursts towards* SHARKY, *as though about to beat him.*

No crying! Don't do a Maurice Macken on it! I'll fucking batter you! Do you hear me?

SHARKY *flinches backwards, blinking, a hand feebly raised.* LOCKHART *laughs.*

(*With disgust.*) Don't make me puke . . .

There is a commotion outside as NICKY *helps* RICHARD *back in through the back door, followed by* IVAN.

RICHARD (*on his way in*). Them friggin' winos! They do my head in!

NICKY. You should've seen it! They ran for their lives!

RICHARD. Good Jaysus, would someone please give me a drink, for the love of God?

NICKY (*grabbing the whiskey bottle to give* RICHARD *a drink*). He blew them out of it! They flew off up the coast! You should have seen it!

IVAN *comes in from the kitchen with a Miller for* NICKY *and a can of Harp for himself.*

RICHARD. But was your man there? My little friend that I fucking hate, with the navy anorak and the big black head of hair on him? He's the worst . . .

NICKY. Yeah, I think there was one like that. He fucking legged it! (*To* SHARKY *and* LOCKHART.) The roars out of this fella . . .

RICHARD. Ah, you have to . . .

NICKY. And then Ivan!

RICHARD. I have Ivan well-trained! You see, they're so shaky and nervy when they get that old meths into them, you can destroy them with a good scream. They think it's the banshee, God help them.

NICKY. Did you see that one was going to the toilet down behind the car?

IVAN. I thought I saw one down in behind . . .

NICKY. That was a woman!

IVAN. Was it?!

RICHARD (*with disgust*). Oh, don't . . . !

NICKY (*bursting out laughing*). It was all going down the back of her leg when she ran and fell over the bin!

RICHARD. Ah stop, will you? They're awful . . .

LOCKHART (*to* IVAN). Is your car alright?

IVAN. Ah . . . it . . . it wasn't my car! I don't have my car with me. I forgot I walked up here in all the excitement.

RICHARD. Ah well, all's well that ends well! Are we gonna play cards?

NICKY (*to* IVAN). Can you see to play cards?

IVAN. I can see to about here. (*He holds his hand up about ten inches from his face.*) After that, it's your guess is as good as mine!

RICHARD. Yeah, you can see the cards . . .

IVAN. I can read the cards . . .

RICHARD. Hey, Shark! Where's all the goodies you promised us that you were banging on about earlier? Get the smoked salmon and the mince pies out and all the Christmas goodies and the crisps and all . . . Are you hungry, Mr Lockhart?

LOCKHART (*looking at* SHARKY). I wouldn't say no.

NICKY (*making a face and touching his stomach*). Them cocktail sausages they were handing out earlier down in Raheny were gone off . . .

RICHARD. Well, Sharky'll get the grub organised. Ivan, pull out that table into the middle, the cards is on the windowsill.

NICKY and IVAN begin to bustle about getting the table ready for cards.

Another beer, Nicky?

NICKY. I have one, I'm good, Richard . . .

RICHARD. Mr Lockhart? Another drop of Irish? Is it there? You can help yourself.

LOCKHART. I'm grand. Sharky's looking after me . . .

NICKY. I'm bursting for a slash, will I run in quickly?

RICHARD. No, run up. There's a better one, Nicky. Sharky! Is that upstairs loo in tip top condition?

SHARKY. Yeah, you know where it is, Nicky.

NICKY. Yup, end of the landing.

NICKY runs up the stairs.

RICHARD. Ivan, there's stout there if you want a stout. I think I might have a stout actually.

IVAN. Good idea.

He goes towards the kitchen.

RICHARD. And don't mind Matt Talbot on the Kaliber there, he can look after himself. Is the table out?

LOCKHART. Here, Richard . . .

LOCKHART helps RICHARD to the table.

RICHARD. Ah, thanks, Mr Lockhart, you're a real gent. And don't mind Sharky's bad humour, he came out backwards and his head has been arseways ever since. Here, give us the cards till I give them a shuffle.

LOCKHART hands the cards to RICHARD. LOCKHART and SHARKY stand looking at each other from opposite ends of the room.

(*Shuffling cards.*) When Ivan comes back now he can cut them for me. (*Laughs.*) I don't know whether these are up or down! I'm in total space here, Mr Lockhart. Wheeee! And when Sharky has the grub for us and Nicky's back down we'll get going. God, I haven't played an old game of poker in so long! I'm really looking forward to it now. Ivan!

IVAN (*off*). Yeah?

RICHARD. Come on till we sort out this money!

IVAN (*off*). I'm coming, Dick! I'm just going to the jacks!

RICHARD. Come on, Nicky! Sit down, Mr Lockhart, sit down. Sharky! Where's Sharky? Sharky, come on! Sharky!! . . . Let's play!!

Blackout.

ACT TWO: MUSIC IN THE SUN

It is many hours later. The room is darker, seemingly lit only by a few lamps, candles and the glow from the stove. The wind is howling outside as a storm lashes the coast. The card game is in progress. RICHARD sits in his armchair which has been pulled nearer to the centre of the room, closer to the table. He has a big box of chocolates nearby and munches one from time to time. To his left sits IVAN, who is at the edge of the table where he can play but also turn easily away from the others to consult strategy with RICHARD. SHARKY sits to IVAN's left and NICKY sits to SHARKY's left. LOCKHART sits at the far end of the table. They are coming to the end of a round of heavy betting. The biggest piles of money are in front of IVAN and LOCKHART. A lot of drink has been consumed; bottles, cans and empty plates are strewn around. IVAN's intoxication is constant, he coasts along, veering neither up into euphoria nor down into depression. It is his efficient life-state, removed, yet heavily present. NICKY, on the other hand, is a euphoric drunk. His genuine love for friends and comrades is freed. While he plays cards he wears wraparound mirror shades like a poker pro. When not playing he sits them on his head. RICHARD, as we have seen, can lurch from sentimentality to vicious insults within seconds. But while all inhibitions may be gone, he remains alert, quick-witted and deeply interested in what goes on around him. LOCKHART is a philosophical drunk, yet prone to deeper maudlin feelings. SHARKY has thus far managed to remain sober . . .

IVAN. Nicky . . .

NICKY. I'm thinking. I'm thinking.

RICHARD. I know. I can hear your brain crunching in your head from over here.

NICKY. Yeah, well, don't be rushing me. What is it again?

RICHARD. Mr Lockhart raised it twenty. We're in. Sharky's bailed.

IVAN. You have to put in forty.

NICKY (*takes a long sharp inhalation and thinks*). Yeah, well, you're bluffing 'cause I saw Richard telling you . . .

RICHARD. Would you go on out of that!

NICKY. Mr Lockhart is being cautious, he raised it twenty, but he's on a roll anyway so he's battering us from a position of strength. (*To* IVAN.) You have nothing.

IVAN (*ironically*). That's right.

NICKY. You have nothing! So stop with the . . . If you didn't have that pile in front of you, I'd have your guts for garters.

RICHARD. Why, what have we got?

NICKY. You've about two hundred and fifty fucking euros in front of you there, Dick.

RICHARD. Yo ho! Santy's come early!

IVAN (*playing down their success*). We're doing alright. We're doing nicely.

NICKY. And half of that is mine. (*With sudden confidence.*) You have fuck all there, Ivan.

IVAN. Well, why don't you make sure?

NICKY. Mr Lockhart has two pair or something.

RICHARD. Well, come on then!

NICKY. I am! (*Seeing and raising.*) Here's your forty. And twenty now to show yous a statement of intent.

RICHARD. Oh ho . . .

NICKY. Now, that shook yous.

IVAN. Mr Lockhart?

LOCKHART. I'll stick around.

He sees NICKY's *twenty.*

IVAN. And we'll have a look.

He sees it too. Pause. NICKY*'s courage seems to wane.*

NICKY (*to* IVAN). What do you have?

IVAN (*to* NICKY). What do you have?

RICHARD. What do we have?

IVAN (*to* NICKY). What do you have?

NICKY (*to* LOCKHART). What do you have?

LOCKHART. Threes.

NICKY. Threes of what?

LOCKHART (*shows his hand*). Three nines.

NICKY. Three nines! You stuck it out with three nines?!

LOCKHART. I enjoy playing. Isn't it worth a go?

NICKY *bursts out laughing.*

RICHARD. What have you got, Nicky?

NICKY. Christmas present. Full house. (*He shows his hand.*)
Fives and kings.

IVAN (*showing his hand*). Kings and sevens.

NICKY. Bollocks!

RICHARD *whoops.*

Ah, that's fucking . . .

LOCKHART. Hard luck, Nicky . . .

NICKY (*to* LOCKHART). What were you doing driving the
pot up the wazoo with three nines?! These lads are cleaning
me out here!

RICHARD. Ah, Nicky . . .

NICKY. Look at me! I'm like Sharky here. I've about thirty-
five euros to me name. This is to do me all through January.

NICKY *gets up and walks over to the stove, restlessly.*

IVAN (*counting his winnings*). Well, Sharky had the right idea. He bailed. He knew.

RICHARD. He has no money!

IVAN. Do you want a stout, Rich?

RICHARD. Sure! Hey! You know what I have in there of course, beside the boiler? There's a drop of Brigid Blake's famous Antrim poteen in there.

IVAN. Oh ho!

RICHARD. Do you ever take a drop, Mr Lockhart?

IVAN *heads towards the kitchen.*

LOCKHART. I will! Why not? Sure I might as well be shit-faced as the way I am!

IVAN (*on his way into the kitchen*). Yo ho!

RICHARD. Good man!

NICKY. Yeah, well leave me out of it . . . Grab us a Miller there, Ivan, would you?

IVAN (*off*). Yeah!

NICKY. Ah, well . . . it's only a game. It's only money, that right, Rich?

RICHARD. Yeah . . . Your money!

NICKY *sighs heavily looking to* LOCKHART *in a silent appeal for understanding.*

NICKY. So, Sharky! You're back! (*Drunkenly placing a hand on* SHARKY*'s shoulder.*) We've missed you! D'you know that?

He turns to LOCKHART, *pointing at* SHARKY *meaninglessly then turns back to* SHARKY.

RICHARD (*insincerely*). Yeah . . . we've all missed you . . .

NICKY. So tell us! Where's this you were working?

SHARKY. Ah, down in Lahinch, County Clare.

NICKY. On the trawlers?

SHARKY. No.

NICKY (*surprised*). No?

SHARKY. No, I was eh . . . (*Glancing at* LOCKHART, *who is smiling at him broadly.*) I was doing a bit of driving for a fella down there.

NICKY. Lahinch? Was I reading somewhere or where was it? That Lahinch is the gay pick-up capital of Europe?

SHARKY. What?

NICKY. So I believe . . .

IVAN *returns with a whiskey bottle full of clear liquid.*

SHARKY. No . . .

RICHARD. Ah Nicky, Lahinch is only a small town, how could it possibly be the gay capital of Europe?

NICKY. Well, I don't know!

RICHARD. The gay capital of Europe is Cork City!

NICKY. Is it?

RICHARD. It very probably is. Are you pouring us a drop of that Moon Juice, Ivan?

IVAN. Will I open it?

RICHARD. Yes.

NICKY. Did you get me a Miller?

IVAN. Did you ask me for one?

NICKY. Yes!

IVAN. Oh sorry, I didn't hear you.

IVAN *goes off towards the kitchen.*

NICKY. Thanks, Ivan. I wouldn't touch that brain blower now if you paid me . . . Look out, Mr Lockhart, you'll be bollixed.

RICHARD. No, he won't! It'll help him play!

NICKY. It will in my arse! Sure Steady Eddie was hallucinating that traffic wardens were coming to arrest him in the snooker club in Harmonstown one morning after he'd been skulling that shite the night before!

RICHARD. Ah, he's a child! Don't mind him, Mr Lockhart.

LOCKHART. No, I'll have a drop.

RICHARD. Good man.

NICKY. Well, I don't mind if you all start losing!

IVAN *returns, making his way to the table to pour some drinks.*

Thanks, Ivan. Good to see you, Shark. Of course you know I'm in a totally new line now myself?

SHARKY. What, you're not doing the babysitting?

NICKY. No, I'm out of the babysitting. I'm out of that this long weather now. Too many trust issues, essentially. Not on my part. No, I'm gone into the cheesemongering business.

SHARKY. Cheesemongering?

IVAN *is pouring some poteen for* RICHARD *and* LOCKHART, *bringing it to them.*

NICKY. Yeah, I've me own counter down the back of Thrifties.

SHARKY. Have you?

NICKY. Yup. I'm only started it, but it could be a whole new empire.

SHARKY. Do you not have to study for years to do something like that?

NICKY (*incredulously*). What!?

SHARKY. I thought you had to study to do cheese and wines and all . . . to do it properly . . .

NICKY. No, you don't! Who told you that?

SHARKY. I don't know. No, I just thought . . .

NICKY. No, you don't! (*He laughs.*) Whoever told you that
now is . . . Ah, poor Sharky!

SHARKY. How's the car?

NICKY. What car?

SHARKY. The Peugeot.

NICKY. Eileen's car?

SHARKY. Well, it's my old car actually.

NICKY. Oh, is it?

SHARKY. Yeah.

NICKY. Did you get a new one?

Pause.

RICHARD. No, he didn't! Sure where would Sharky get a new
car? (*Raising his glass of poteen.*) Your health, Mr Lockhart!

NICKY. Say goodbye to it!

LOCKHART. No, this is smooth!

NICKY. Yeah, you think . . .

LOCKHART. You know this is the only time of the year I
really enjoy? A game of cards on Christmas Eve, sure
where would you get it?

RICHARD. Absolutely!

IVAN. You play a lot of cards, Mr Lockhart?

LOCKHART. Well . . . I do at Christmas! Boys, I've played
cards in public houses, shebeens, hotel bar rooms, suburban
boozers – anywhere! Three, four in the morning, nobody
there, only a few auld lads in their shirt sleeves, tidying up
while they watch some poor fucking eejit play it all away . . .
Houses! Little houses . . . on Christmas Eve . . . in the
middle of nowhere I've played. Out on the Western seaboard,
but mostly in the East. Ah, I've played everywhere! You
name it! In Garda barracks . . . Sharky. Up in amazing
Georgian rooms with wonderful evocative gilt mirrors and

beautiful windows towering out on to bountiful trees – in the middle of Dublin, or London, in the city, yup. A school or two I've played in. In my time. Always late. It's always so late . . . Time deepens and slows down somehow in a card game. It could be any moment. It's always the same moment . . . Where do I know you from, Ivan?

IVAN. Ha?

LOCKHART. Have we played cards?

SHARKY. No, I don't think you have . . .

IVAN. Yeah, we might of . . .

LOCKHART. You're the fella won the boat that time in a card game, Nicky was telling me . . .

NICKY. Yeah.

IVAN (*modestly*). Well . . .

RICHARD. No, he did, that's right.

IVAN (*to* RICHARD). Do you remember that, Dick?

RICHARD. I sure do! 'The Briquette Queen.'

NICKY. Forty grand's worth of boat, Mr Lockhart!

IVAN. Yeah, but I sold it for twelve. I didn't want it! What would I want with a fucking boat?

NICKY. It only would've cost him money anyway . . .

IVAN. I sold it for twelve grand up in the Cock tavern in Howth – Do you remember, Richard? Best Christmas ever!

RICHARD. Ah, brilliant. It was brilliant!

NICKY. You could never top that!

IVAN. I lost it all in three weeks, Mr Lockhart. Betting in the bookies in Baldoyle and practically living in Doyle's Lounge. I was eating so much fish and chips and battered sausages at all weird hours and I saw fuck-all daylight . . .

NICKY. This is all true!

IVAN. . . . that I ended up getting the runs so bad and I was so
dehydrated the doctor wouldn't let me out of the house for
four whole days!

RICHARD, NICKY *and* IVAN *are laughing* . . .

It was unbelievable! It was an absolutely unbelievable
Christmas. Do you remember all the stars we saw that
Stephen's Night, Nicky?

NICKY (*too beautiful to describe*). Aw!

IVAN. Yeah, but you panic though when it starts to run right
down. Oh Jaysus, if Karen had've known I'd had all that . . .
Oh! (*He shudders*). Had to get rid of it.

LOCKHART. Yeah, and you won it just in a card game in a
house?

IVAN. Yeah, won it off a total nutcase that killed himself not
long after. He drowned after driving his lorry off the end of
the pier in Howth.

NICKY. 'The Briquette Queen.'

IVAN. He had a business delivering peat briquettes . . .

RICHARD. Oh, he was a nasty piece of work, Mr Lockhart . . .

NICKY. Aw, he was a real bollocks!

LOCKHART. Yeah? God, that's a great story. But you know
what I was wondering, after Nicky told me about it, I
wanted to ask you . . . Look at Sharky looking at me
suspiciously there . . . no, I was just wondering, with the
stakes so high – a forty grand boat, like – I was wondering
what you had in the pot that he was betting his boat against
you?

IVAN. Ha?

LOCKHART. No, just what did you have in the pot to put up
against his boat? I'm assuming there couldn't have been
forty grand in the pot. In a card game like the way we're
playing now . . . What did you have, that he wanted . . . ?

IVAN *looks at* NICKY. *Pause.*

SHARKY. Here, look, are we gonna play here?

LOCKHART. You don't have to tell me . . .

RICHARD. It was stupid! Your man was out of it! They were all elephants!

NICKY. He was a lunatic! He was acting the bollocks. Ivan took him down fair and square and . . .

LOCKHART. It was something to do with that hotel down in Wicklow, was it?

Long pause.

SHARKY (*to* LOCKHART). What are you doing?

LOCKHART. You told me something about that, Nicky, didn't you? About Ivan and what was it? The Ardlawn Hotel?

NICKY (*guiltily*). No . . .

RICHARD (*disappointed*). Nicky . . .

NICKY. I didn't . . .

SHARKY. Let's just play, will we? That's got nothing to do with anything.

LOCKHART. What was the name of those two families?

IVAN (*in a dark place*). The Murdochs and the Kavanaghs.

LOCKHART. That's right . . .

RICHARD. That was all in the news. Ivan was completely exonerated . . .

NICKY. It was inconclusive . . .

SHARKY. Yeah. Hey, look . . . Can we just get on with the . . .

SHARKY *takes a sharp intake of breath and puts his hand to his head in sudden, immense pain.*

NICKY. Are you alright, Shark?

SHARKY (*blinking*). Yeah, no, I'm . . .

RICHARD. Leave him alone. He just needs a drink. That whole thing was an open and shut case, Mr Lockhart . . .

LOCKHART. What happened? There was a fire . . . ?

IVAN. Yeah, well . . . It was twenty odd years ago. It was more . . .

NICKY. Ancient history . . .

IVAN. I was working in the Ardlawn. I was doing a bit of portering and bit of night-portering . . .

RICHARD. Ivan was completely exonerated.

NICKY. There was no blame.

IVAN. No, they had to investigate it. I had . . . you see I had burned my hand on the ring of the cooker when I was . . . I was heating some beans . . . it was very late and . . . (*Pause.*) This was all in the papers!

LOCKHART. Yeah . . . but it can really hang over a man, something like that . . .

IVAN. Well, yeah, the . . . this fella with the boat, the briquette king. He wanted to play for . . .

NICKY. He was a wanker.

IVAN. The bet was that he could . . . if he won, he wanted to ask me . . . about it. I don't know . . .

LOCKHART. To give him the truth.

Pause.

IVAN. Yeah . . .

NICKY. It was a ridiculous fucking bet . . . He was a sick fucking eejit and that's all that was going on. And he got his comeuppance!

RICHARD. He's gone and good luck to him. He was a bully.

LOCKHART. High stakes, Ivan . . .

IVAN. Yeah . . . well I'd a strong hand.

LOCKHART. Yeah. I knew there had to be something . . . You don't mind talking about it . . .

Pause.

NICKY. I hate that fucking poteen! The fucking smell of it, even!

RICHARD. Ah, stop giving out! Are we gonna play cards?
There's too much Auld Lang Syne going on around here
and not enough cards!

NICKY. Yeah, well, let's play, come on!

RICHARD. Whose deal is it? Sharky! You deal!

LOCKHART. Yes! We haven't hardly had a burst out of Sharky
tonight at all!

RICHARD. Ah, Sharky could never play cards!

NICKY (*gathering up the cards to give* SHARKY). I've seen
Sharky win.

LOCKHART. Maybe he's preoccupied.

RICHARD. Ah, he's always preoccupied . . .

NICKY. Come on. Two euros to play. Maybe this is Sharky's
hand.

RICHARD. Give us a drop of that holy water, Ivan, till we
bless ourselves.

NICKY. Little threes is all I need.

SHARKY *shuffles the cards to deal. Everyone puts in two
euros.* IVAN *puts in four, to cover himself and* RICHARD,
then he gets up to pour a drink for RICHARD.

IVAN. Richard . . .

RICHARD (*to* IVAN). Good man. (*Raising glass.*) Mr Lockhart?

LOCKHART. I will! Thank you, Ivan.

RICHARD. Hey, Mr Lockhart . . .

LOCKHART *looks at* RICHARD *who points to his head
and makes a whistling sound to indicate the effect of the
poteen.*

LOCKHART. I know! I'm fucking slipping in and out of time
zones here. I thought it was last Christmas there for a
minute!

RICHARD. Yes! That's right!

IVAN *goes to pour a drink for* LOCKHART.

NICKY. Yeah, well leave me out of it. I want to stay here in this Christmas and beat the shite out of yous now with this hand. I can feel it in me waters. Little threes there now, Sharky. Get us a Miller there, Ivan, will you?

IVAN *goes to get a beer.*

IVAN. Do you want another Seven-Up, Shark?

SHARKY. Nah, I'm alright . . .

RICHARD. Oh, threes is a beaut . . .

NICKY. That's my killer hand, is three threes.

RICHARD. Yeah: I love three tens. Three tens is my . . .

LOCKHART. Ah, a ten is like a shining tower. It's like the Twentieth Century. It's solid. It looms at you, yeah?

RICHARD. Absolutely.

NICKY. Well, I also like to see an eight. Give me a pair of eights for starters and I'm . . .

RICHARD (*dismissively*). Ah, eight! Eight is sneaky . . . Look at it! What is it? Eight! It's not a ten, it's almost as bad as a nine . . .

LOCKHART. Well, nine can have a certain symmetry to it.

NICKY. Oh, three threes is a lovely little hand. It's like a little grenade.

RICHARD. And seven . . .

LOCKHART. Oh, seven is deep.

NICKY (*to* IVAN, *who has returned with beers for* NICKY *and himself*). We're talking about numbers.

IVAN (*unconvinced*). Ah, seven is only my hole. Give me a four.

SHARKY. Yeah . . .

IVAN. Four is where you build your house.

They have all picked up their cards and peruse them.

LOCKHART (*to* IVAN). Do you not have two fours in front of you there?

IVAN. That's a secret, Mr Lockhart.

NICKY. Ah, nice try! Mr Lockhart is no slouch!

RICHARD. Well, neither is Ivan! How are we doing? Who's it to?

SHARKY. Ivan?

IVAN. Ah, check . . .

SHARKY. Nicky?

NICKY. Eh . . . I'll check for a minute.

SHARKY. Mr Lockhart . . .

LOCKHART. Ah, sure we'll make it interesting anyway. (*Putting in coins.*) Three euros.

RICHARD. Will we stick around for three euros, Ivan?

IVAN. We'll see what happens.

He puts in coins.

SHARKY. Nicky?

NICKY. Ah, we'll hang around.

Sees the bet.

SHARKY. And I'll have a look. (*Sees it and picks up the deck to deal.*) Ivan?

IVAN. Eh . . . Three please, Sharky.

SHARKY *deals him three cards.*

LOCKHART. Little pair of fours there, Ivan?

RICHARD. Don't tell him nothing!

IVAN. I'm not . . .

SHARKY. Nicky.

NICKY. Eh . . . two . . .

SHARKY deals him two cards. NICKY suddenly throws down one more card.

No, three . . .

SHARKY. You sure?

NICKY. Yeah, three, thanks.

SHARKY (*deals another card to* NICKY). Mr Lockhart?

LOCKHART. Just one, please, Sharky.

Reactions to this around the table. SHARKY deals him a card.

RICHARD. Just the one, Mr Lockhart?

LOCKHART. Just the one . . .

NICKY. Ah, he's on a kamikaze. What is it? A run? Flush? Did you get it?

LOCKHART. Maybe it's four of a kind.

RICHARD. Maybe it's total bollocks.

LOCKHART. Maybe . . .

SHARKY. And I'll take three. To you, Mr Lockhart.

LOCKHART. Ah, we'll keep the dream alive. Sure, five euros.

Puts in money.

RICHARD. Oh, look out . . .

SHARKY. Ivan?

IVAN. Ehm . . . We'll hang on.

Sees the bet.

RICHARD. We'll hang on for a minute . . .

SHARKY. Nicky?

NICKY. Ah, we'll go along for the ride. (*He sees it.*) And we'll make it interesting. Ten euros.

He raises the bet. Reactions around the table . . .

RICHARD. Oh, now!

SHARKY. Mr Lockhart?

LOCKHART. I'll see you . . . With ten.

Raises the bet further still.

RICHARD. Oh now, here! What are we doing? Ivan!

NICKY (*to* LOCKHART). You fucker . . .

IVAN *leans over to whisper to* RICHARD, *who listens intently . . .*

RICHARD. Ah, fold, for fuck's sake! Would you? Jaysus . . .

IVAN (*throws his hand in*). We're gone.

SHARKY. Nicky?

NICKY (*considers* LOCKHART). I'll see you.

Puts in ten.

RICHARD. You're a fucking eejit . . .

NICKY. Hold your horses. Stranger things have happened at sea . . .

RICHARD (*dismissively*). Yeah, right . . .

LOCKHART. Sharky?

RICHARD. Don't be a hero now, Sharky . . .

SHARKY (*considering his hand*). So what is it?

NICKY. It's twenty-eight for you to play, Shark. And I'd advise you to tread warily against what I have here now . . .

RICHARD. Easy now, Sharky. I'm not keeping you in pocket money for the whole of next month now, right?

SHARKY. Twenty-eight. (*He sees it and reaches into his pocket, taking some money out*). With twenty-five.

RICHARD. What!?

IVAN. Ah, let him play, Rich.

LOCKHART. Brave man . . .

NICKY. To you, Mr Lockhart . . .

LOCKHART. I'm in.

He sees the bet. NICKY *looks at his cards . . .*

IVAN. Nicky . . .

NICKY. I'm thinking. I'm thinking. I'm thinking. I'm thinking.

RICHARD. I thought I smelled something burning . . .

NICKY. Ha ha . . . (*To* LOCKHART, *putting money in.*) Come on! What do you have?

Pause.

LOCKHART (*showing his hand*). I've nothing.

NICKY. You bastard! What were you doing?!

LOCKHART. I'm playing the game!

NICKY (*derisively*). The game! You fucking eejit. That's that poteen. I told you . . .

IVAN. It could be yours, Nicky . . .

RICHARD. It better not be!

IVAN. Go on, Nicky! What do you have?

Pause.

NICKY. Ah, I've even less nothing. I've a hand of feet. Half a run. I knew he (*Lockhart*) had nothing. I thought it'd be too pricey for Sharky. I thought he was having us on. What have you got Shark, two pair or some fucking thing . . .

SHARKY. Not even. One pair.

NICKY. One pair?! (*He grabs* SHARKY's *cards.*) Two fucking fours!?

IVAN. It still beats you.

LOCKHART. Nicely played, Sharky . . .

NICKY *throws the cards on the table and stands up.*

NICKY. A hundred euros with two fours!

He paces around, going towards the stove.

SHARKY. Your deal, Nicky . . .

NICKY *kicks a pile of newspapers.*

NICKY. Bollocks!

RICHARD. Oy! Oy! Nicky, don't destroy the place.

NICKY. No, no. I'm sorry, Richard.

IVAN. Nice one, Sharky . . .

NICKY (*taking money from his wallet*). What were we all doing? (*To* LOCKHART.) You had nothing!? I had fuck all! And Sharky wins a hundred euros with two fucking fours!

LOCKHART. Luck of the draw.

NICKY. What were you doing raising all the time?

LOCKHART. You were raising as well.

NICKY. Ah, I was only having a go! Here, give us some change there, Ivan.

LOCKHART. It's only money . . .

NICKY *goes to* IVAN'*s pile to get some smaller denominations, throwing two twenty-euro notes down.*

RICHARD. Ah, hard luck, Nicky, sure it's only a bit of fun . . .

NICKY. I won't be having much more fun at this rate . . .

RICHARD. You could never bluff, Nicky. That's just something you can't . . .

IVAN (*pointing at* SHARKY). You see him? King of the bluffers.

RICHARD. Who, Sharky?

IVAN. Yeah.

RICHARD. Yeah, well, that's only because he has a recklessness in his heart which is the undoing and ruination of his whole life.

IVAN. Not tonight.

RICHARD. Yeah? Just wait. Ah, cheer up, Nicky.

NICKY. Yeah, well, give me a few minutes . . . ! That's a harsh lesson there now.

LOCKHART. Only kind that works, Nicky.

IVAN. Well, Sharky's around for another few hands in anyway . . .

RICHARD. He should quit while he's ahead.

LOCKHART. Don't worry, Nicky. I'm gonna take Sharky down.

NICKY. Can I bet on it?

LOCKHART. Nothing surer.

RICHARD. Ah, would you come on and deal the cards and stop moaning. You'll probably trounce us all this time out.

NICKY (*taking the cards to give them a shuffle*). I hope so!

RICHARD (*handing box of sweets to* IVAN). Here, Ivan, pass them around.

IVAN. Oh, nice one!

A mobile phone is ringing somewhere . . .

RICHARD. What's that music?

NICKY. Oh bollocks! That's my phone!

RICHARD. Oh, here's trouble . . .

IVAN. I'm not here . . .

NICKY *goes to his jacket and rummages for his phone . . .*

NICKY. It's Eileen!

IVAN. Well, whoever it is, I'm not here.

They all wait as NICKY *stands looking at his phone.*

NICKY. I'm gonna have to answer this, Dick.

RICHARD. Well, would you answer the Jaysus thing and stop driving us all around the fucking twist!

NICKY answers it.

NICKY (*very innocently*). Hello?

The others are listening.

Hi hon. What? No! No, I'm just visiting poor Richard to see if he . . . No. No, Sharky's here. Yeah, no he's here. He's not even drinking. And I'm only . . . I'm just having a very quick bottle of Miller. No, I swear to God, he isn't! What? Yeah, no I'll be back. No, don't try lifting it down yourself . . . No, no I'll do it! (*He drifts upstage towards the staircase and upstairs out of earshot of the others.*) No, I'll be there! What's wrong with you? It's Christmas, Eileen! What? Hold on, just let me . . .

He is gone.

RICHARD. Trouble in paradise.

IVAN. Don't talk to me about trouble in paradise! Here, will I put on some music?

RICHARD. Oh yes! Good idea! Good idea!

IVAN wanders over to the stereo . . .

LOCKHART. Hey, hold on, are we not gonna . . . ? (*Unsaid 'play'.*)

RICHARD. Music to soothe the soul. What kind of music do you like, Mr Lockhart?

LOCKHART. I don't really like music.

IVAN surfs up the dial on the tuner and finds some softly-played, festive, perhaps choral, music . . .

RICHARD. How can you not like music? Any music?

LOCKHART. I don't like any music.

RICHARD. Do you hear that, Ivan? Mr Lockhart doesn't like any music!

IVAN. Sure, that's impossible.

RICHARD. That's what I would've thought.

LOCKHART. No, you see . . . I can't hear it.

IVAN. What, are you tone-deaf?

LOCKHART. No, no, I just don't like the sound. You see, to me it's just an ugly noise.

RICHARD. Dear God! That's a terrible affliction. Sure you can hardly escape music!

IVAN. What? Like, do you want me to turn it off?

LOCKHART. If you don't mind.

IVAN *stands there, hoping* LOCKHART *will relent.*

That would be most agreeable.

IVAN *goes and turns off the music. Pause.*

RICHARD. Lordy, lordy, lordy, lordy, lordy, lordy, lordy, lordy, lordy, would you listen to that wind? God, I had an awful dream the other night. I dreamt I could see. I dreamt that I woke up and I could see and that being blind had been a dream. And I dreamt the sun was shining in through the window there, and there, just sitting on the windowsill, was a bluebottle looking at me. You ever notice about those things? The whole head is nearly their eyes. Two big black footballs on the whole two sides of their head. And I was just staring at him and he was just staring at me – as much as you can tell if he's 'looking' at you at all . . . 'What does he think of me?' I was wondering, as we were kind of . . . communing with each other there. And there was such . . . comfort, in his blank unseeing regard for me, Mr Lockhart. You just know that God is in a fly, don't you? The very existence and the amazing design in something so small and intricate as a bluebottle – it's God's revelation really, isn't it? Don't you feel that?

LOCKHART. Well . . . except that they seem to like the taste of shit so much, don't they?

RICHARD. Ah, that only adds to their intrigue . . .

LOCKHART. If you say so.

RICHARD. Well I do! I do say so! And . . . But then I had the terrible misfortune to wake up and . . . and I realised I couldn't see. And I kind of . . . I kind of panicked. I didn't know if it was night, or day, or what the hell it was or where I was. And I didn't want to call out to Sharky, because in case I woke him, his moods do be bad enough! And I . . . or turn on the radio in case I woke him, but I got my bearings. I was down here and I thought, 'If I can get a drop of whiskey, the old panic may subside.' But then, of course, I fell in the fucking kitchen door and I made such a clatter that Sharky woke up anyway! Didn't you?

SHARKY. Yeah, well, I wasn't asleep. But Jaysus . . . I thought someone was breaking in. Bottles smashing all over the floor . . .

RICHARD. Yeah! What was it? It was . . .

SHARKY. It was five o'clock in the bleeding morning.

RICHARD. Yeah, well, we were up then, weren't we?

SHARKY. Yeah.

RICHARD. Then your man (*Sharky*) wants to give me a bath! (*Pronounced 'bat'.*)

LOCKHART. A what?

IVAN *goes round with the poteen topping up their drinks . . .*

RICHARD. A bat! He wants to wash me! And bathe me, the fucking . . . (*Unsaid 'eejit'.*)

LOCKHART. Well, he's trying to be what's known as 'a good person'.

RICHARD. Well he should give up! (*He laughs.*) Hey, Sharky, (*Touching his groin.*) what about that . . .

SHARKY (*remembering with disgust*). Oh . . . !

RICHARD. Ivan, there was a . . . what would you call it, Sharky?

SHARKY. I don't want to talk about it.

RICHARD. It was like a lump of . . . up here at the top of me leg where the crease meets the . . .

SHARKY. Aw, would you fucking stop, Richard?

RICHARD. It was hard, now. And deeply . . . embedded in the . . .

SHARKY. Ah, Richard!

RICHARD. Like either congealed . . . or . . . The smell when Sharky started rubbing it!

NICKY *descends.*

SHARKY. Richard!

RICHARD. And the fucking pain of it . . . Sharky going at it with the nailbrush! And the smell!

NICKY. What's this?

RICHARD. Nicky, you'd be interested in this, I had this . . .

SHARKY. No, come on, that's it now. Jesus Christ!

RICHARD (*angrily*). Ah, I'm only trying tell a fucking story here, Jim, what's the matter with you, for Jaysus' sake?! (*Short pause, to* NICKY.) I'll tell you later . . .

Short pause.

NICKY. Well, I've got about an hour's parole, so let's get on with the cards because if I want to have any chance of . . .

There is a sudden loud bang at the back door out in the kitchen. They all fall silent, listening.

What was that?

RICHARD (*getting up*). That's them fucking winos! Where's me stick? Ivan!

SHARKY. Ah, Rich, come on . . . don't be . . .

NICKY goes into the kitchen, peering out the back door into the gloom.

RICHARD. Don't fucking start now, Sharky! You don't know what I have to live with! I'm sorry, Mr Lockhart, we have an awful problem with these winos out in the lane, come on, Ivan!

IVAN. They're probably gone, they just . . .

NICKY. I think they must have thrown something or . . .

IVAN. Put the light on out there, Nicky.

RICHARD *has a hold of* IVAN.

RICHARD. Come on, Ivan. Come on, Nicky. Open that back door for me.

NICKY. Hey, hold on, is there something I can . . . ?

RICHARD. There's an old golf club in there beside the jacks door, Nicky.

IVAN. Put the light on out there, Nicky, will you?

NICKY *finds the golf club and hits a light in the back garden.*

NICKY. Hold on now, Rich, now I don't see anyone.

RICHARD. Come on, we'll get them in the lane.

SHARKY. Richard, put your coat on, will you?

RICHARD. Ah, we're alright, we'll just chase them off.

IVAN. They'll be gone I'd say anyway.

NICKY *opens the back door and goes out into the wind,* RICHARD *and* IVAN *following.* RICHARD *does a native Indian whooping sound by vibrating his open palm in front of his mouth while letting out a high-pitched shout.*

RICHARD (*going*). Keep a hold of me now, Ivan!

NICKY (*off*). Hey, mind with that stick, will ya?

RICHARD (*off*). Sorry, Nicky!

The back door shuts. SHARKY *and* LOCKHART *are alone. Pause.*

LOCKHART. Well, Sharky. You ready to come with me?

SHARKY. You haven't beaten me yet.

LOCKHART (*getting up to pour himself more poteen*). No, not yet, I'm enjoying myself too much! I'll hammer you now in this next hand. And then I'll take you right through the old hole in the wall.

As LOCKHART *pours himself a drink, he sways and steadies himself against the table.*

Whoops.

SHARKY. Mind you don't fall.

LOCKHART. Well, to tell you the truth, I never drink this much.

SHARKY. Yeah, well, welcome to our house.

LOCKHART. Mmm. Your brother . . . He's a real . . . believer, isn't he?

SHARKY *shrugs.* LOCKHART *stands with his drink and raises his free hand to look at it in the light.*

I hate these stupid insect bodies you have. (*He switches his drink from one hand to another*). This fucker is left-handed! (*Looking down at his legs.*) I mean, what is it? What are human beings? Two balloons – that's your lungs and an annoying little whistle at the top where the air comes out – that's your voice . . . (*Pause. Bitterly.*) I mean what have you got that I haven't?! (*Short pause.*) I'm talking to you, Love's Young Dream! What have you got? Ha? You all age and wither before me like dead flowers in a bright window! You're nothing! Me? I live in the stars above St Anne's park! Thousands of Christmas Eves I've seen! I'm so old . . . and thousands more I'll see; maybe millions! I'm the very power that keeps us apart! Isn't that worth saving? (*Beat.*) Evidently not. No, he loves you. He loves all you insects . . . (*Lost and distant.*) Figure that one out.

Pause.

SHARKY. What'll to happen to me? If I lose.

LOCKHART. When you lose.

SHARKY. If I lose.

LOCKHART. You're going to Hell.

Short pause.

SHARKY. What is it?

LOCKHART. What's Hell? (*He gives a little laugh.*) Hell is . . . (*He stares gloomily.*) Well, you know, Sharky, when you're walking round and round the city and the street lights have all come on and it's cold. Or you're standing outside a shop where you were hanging around reading the magazines, pretending to buy one 'cause you've no money and nowhere to go and your feet are like blocks of ice in those stupid little slip-on shoes you bought for chauffeuring. And you see all the people who seem to live in another world all snuggled up together in the warmth of a tavern or a cosy little house, and you just walk and walk and walk and you're on your own and nobody knows who you are. And you don't know anyone and you're trying not to hassle people or beg, because you're trying not to drink, and you're hoping you won't meet anyone you know because of the blistering shame that rises up in your face and you have to turn away because you know you can't even deal with the thought that someone might love you, because of all the pain you always cause.

Well, that's a fraction of the self-loathing you feel in Hell, except it's worse. Because there truly is no one to love you. Not even Him. (*He points to the sky.*) He lets you go. Even He's sick of you. You're locked in a space that's smaller than a coffin. And it's lying a thousand miles down, under the bed of a vast, icy, pitch-black sea. You're buried alive in there. And it's so cold that you can feel your angry tears freezing in your eye lashes and your very bones ache with deep perpetual agony and you think, 'I must be going to die . . .'

But you never die. You never even sleep, because every few minutes you're gripped by a claustrophobic panic and you get so frightened you squirm uselessly against the stone walls and the heavy lid you've banged your head off a million times and your heart beats so fast against your ribs you think, 'I must be going to die . . .' But of course . . . you

never will. Because of what you did. And what you didn't
do.

Pause. SHARKY *stares into his bleak eternal fate.*

That's where I am too, Sharky. I know you see me here in
this man's clothes, but that's where I really am . . . Out on
that sea. (*Short pause.*) Oh, you'd have loved Heaven, Sharky.
It's unbelievable! Everyone feels peaceful! (*He laughs.*)
Everyone feels at such peace! Simply to exist there is to
know an exquisite, trance-like bliss, because your mind is
at one with the infinite!

(*Darker.*) At a certain point each day, music plays. It seems
to emanate from the very sun itself. Not so much a tune as a
heartbreakingly beautiful vibration in the sunlight shining
down on and through all the souls. It's so moving you
wonder how you could ever have doubted anything as you
think back on this painful life which is just a sad distant
memory. Time just slips away in Heaven, Sharky. But not
for you. No. You are about to find out that time is more
measureless and bigger and blacker and so much more
boundless than you could ever have thought possible with
your puny broken mind.

SHARKY *looks down forlornly.*

Poor old Sharky. You've really got it for her, haven't you?

SHARKY. Who?

LOCKHART (*derisively*). Who! The wife of that fella you
were working for down in Lahinch.

SHARKY *looks away.*

. . . That sent you all those CDs this morning! (*Derisively.*)
'Who . . . ?' Trust you to blow it, Sharky. Trust you. That's
how I know you'll be coming with me tonight. I know
you'll lose this next hand. Because you always make a pig's
mickey of everything.

SHARKY *seems to ponder his whole life for a moment,
then goes to the bottle of poteen and pours himself a huge*

measure. He begins to drink it perfunctorily with one hand on his hip . . .

That's it, Sharky, good man. Drink yourself up on to the next shelf in the basement. Drink to where possibility feels infinite and your immortality feels strong.

SHARKY, *having drained his glass, joylessly pours another.*

That's it . . . Genius! You poor, stupid bastard.

SHARKY. Why don't you give it a rest?

LOCKHART. The condemned man's last meal. A big glass of hooch!

SHARKY (*snapping at* LOCKHART). I said, give it rest, will ya?

LOCKHART (*fumbling towards* SHARKY, *holding out his glass*). Here, give me one.

SHARKY (*shuffling away*). Get it yourself.

LOCKHART. Oy, oy, oy oy!

SHARKY *drinks while* LOCKHART *looks at him, unsure for a moment . . . We hear a commotion as the others return to the kitchen through the back door. They are laughing.*

NICKY (*wandering in to get a drink*). They'd scarpered! They were gone!

RICHARD (*coming through with* IVAN). We chased them off! Another battle to us. The generals prevail! Ivan, would you please pour us a sharpener to warm us up? Mr Lockhart? Are you alright for a . . . ?

LOCKHART. I don't know . . . This poor brain can't cope, I don't think!

RICHARD. Would you go on out of that? Have a stout! Ivan, are you alright? Ivan fell.

NICKY (*laughs*). Ivan wrecked himself!

IVAN. Ah, I walked right into the basin of dirty water Sharky left out there! Me socks are ringing!

RICHARD. You fucking eejit!

IVAN (*going towards kitchen*). Ah, I'll take these off. I'll deal with it later . . .

RICHARD. You gobaloon . . . And Sharky, what were you doing leaving a basin of water in the laneway? (*Imploring the heavens.*) Lord, I'm surrounded by ninnies! Deliver me!

NICKY. Oh, I'll tell yous, Richard's blood is up!

RICHARD. What?

NICKY. He's missed his mill with the winos!

RICHARD. Excuse me?

NICKY. You were gunning for a fight, so you were, go on out of that!

RICHARD. Yeah, right! Sure, how could I be? I'm blind, Nicky, actually, you know?

NICKY. Go on out of that! That never stopped you! (*Spies* SHARKY *pouring a drink.*) You having a Christmas nip, Sharky?

RICHARD (*ears pricking up at this*). Ha?

IVAN *falls in the kitchen door with a crash, trying to get his socks off.*

NICKY. Wo! Easy there, Ivan! Are you alright?

IVAN (*off*). Yah . . .

RICHARD. So . . . Is Sharky back among the living, yeah?

LOCKHART. He's just trying to kill the pain.

RICHARD. Mr Lockhart, take it from me, Sharky will never kill all that pain. He'd have to drink Lough Derg dry, God help him!

They all laugh except SHARKY, *who continues to drink perfunctorily . . .* IVAN *wanders back in, barefoot, from the kitchen, drinking a beer.* NICKY *brings* RICHARD *a drink.*

Ah, at last! Hey, Cheers, Sharky! (*He raises his glass, needling* SHARKY.) Welcome back!

SHARKY *just looks at* RICHARD *darkly.* NICKY, IVAN *and* LOCKHART *look at* SHARKY.

SHARKY. Yeah, Cheers, Richard . . .

NICKY *and* IVAN *relax but . . .*

RICHARD. Ah, clink me glass, will ya?

SHARKY *reluctantly goes and clinks his glass against* RICHARD's.

Good man. Drink up. Mr Lockhart, it's a well-known fact in this whole area that my brother has that rare gift which is, unfortunately, the opposite to whatever the Midas touch was.

NICKY. Ah, Richard . . .

RICHARD. No, no . . . I'm going to say something positive. I believe that Sharky has potential. Yes. I believe he can change.

LOCKHART. Ah, well, that's sweet . . . Isn't that nice, Sharky?

NICKY (*moving to the table*). Yeah, lovely. Come on, are we gonna play cards?

RICHARD. You ever see an old couple going down the street, Mr Lockhart? An old couple who've been married for a million years, going along the road to the shops or to mass, with their grey, dead faces?

LOCKHART. Yes.

RICHARD. Like some ghastly ancient brother and sister. Nothing to say to each other any more or ever again except to snap the fucking head off each other for not putting the jelly back in the fridge or some fucking shite, you ever see that? Don't tell me they were always like that! Don't tell me they haven't changed! 'Cause I won't believe it! No, I believe in Sharky. He can change. I believe that he can change back to . . .

SHARKY. Back to what?

NICKY. Will I deal?

IVAN. Yeah, go on, Nicky, deal . . .

LOCKHART. Hold on, Sharky wants to ask something . . .

RICHARD. What did you say?

SHARKY. Back to what? I can change back to what?

NICKY. Ah, lads . . .

RICHARD. Well . . . How about back to the little fella that always had a tune on his lips and had integrity, and wasn't a sneaky little fucker who broke his mother's heart. How's that for starters?

NICKY. Ah, Richard, come on . . .

RICHARD. Back to that! You see, I remember, Mr Lockhart, when it was all fields all's around here . . . all around all up to Donaghmede, all up to Sutton, all up to Howth. All fields, Mr Lockhart. All farms, Nicky.

NICKY. Yeah, well my roots are in Ballyfermot.

RICHARD. Our mother was a wonderful woman! (*He suddenly stands to attention.*) Our father was a fine man. A tough man. He was devoted to his greyhounds! He lived for them! Great with his fists.

LOCKHART. That's fascinating . . .

RICHARD. Yes. No, our mother, God rest her, she only ever had one problem in her life. Sharky. Yes . . .

NICKY. Ah, Richard, come on, that's the poteen talking. Sharky, sit down till we play . . .

RICHARD. He upset her that much, she hit him with a chair and broke it one night, Mr Lockhart. I witnessed it.

NICKY. Ah, come on, Dick, come on, Sharky . . . let's not have the yearly . . .

SHARKY. What's your point, Richard?

RICHARD. Ha?

IVAN. Come on, Shark . . .

SHARKY. What? Did you want me to stay? And live here with you and them? And all the fucking rows all the time, and all the fucking drink?

RICHARD. You never needed anyone to show you how to drink!

SHARKY. 'Cause would you have got the house then?

RICHARD. What!

NICKY. Ah, lads, for fuck's sake . . .

LOCKHART. No, wait, let Sharky finish.

SHARKY. I am finished.

RICHARD. What do you mean would I have got the house then? How dare you?

SHARKY. You think you've always got it all figured out. Look at you.

RICHARD. What do you mean 'Look at me?' Look at you!!

SHARKY. Yeah well, don't worry about it. Because you know what? You're gonna get what you want.

NICKY. Ah, lads . . .

SHARKY. 'Cause I'm leaving here tonight and I'll be gone and that'll be the end of it.

NICKY. Ah, Sharky . . .

SHARKY (*forcefully*). And you can walk into the walls and spill Paddy Powers all down your horrible filthy whiskers and sit in your own stink 'cause you don't even know what day it is or what time it is. And then they'll stick you in some home out in Blanchardstown or somewhere where you won't even get a drink, how does that sound?

RICHARD. You're being completely unreasonable!

SHARKY. Am I? Just watch!

NICKY. Come on, Sharky, you don't mean it . . .

SHARKY. Yeah? Tell them, Mr Lockhart, or whatever your fucking name is, go on, tell him! Tell him!

NICKY *is on his feet, trying to pacify* SHARKY.

NICKY. Sharky . . . come on . . . it's alright . . .

SHARKY. Take your fucking hands off me, I'll give you such a box in the fucking head!

IVAN. Wo, wo . . . Sharky . . .

NICKY. Hey, easy, Shark . . .

SHARKY. You're only a fucking scumbag.

NICKY. What?

SHARKY. You heard me, you sponger.

IVAN *is also on his feet.*

IVAN. Ah, Sharky, now, come on . . .

SHARKY. Eileen is far too good for a fucking scumhead like you. Always on the mooch . . .

NICKY. Hey! Don't be having a go at me! (*He rolls up his sleeve to show* SHARKY *a tattoo.*) Read that! What does that say! Eileen! And that? Eileen! I look after Eileen and the kids!

IVAN. Ah, lads!

NICKY. At least I don't be getting into mills all the time and getting barred out of pubs all over the place! At least I don't be waking up screaming and roaring at all hours of the night having bad dreams and freaking the kids out and waking the whole place up!

RICHARD. That's right!

SHARKY. What?

NICKY. Sure everybody knows! You're a nutcase, Sharky! Everybody knows!

SHARKY *enters an inarticulate rage and throws a punch at* NICKY. NICKY *defends himself, pushing* SHARKY *backwards.* IVAN *manages to get a hold of* SHARKY *and restrains him.*

RICHARD. What's going on? Sharky! Calm down!

SHARKY *tries to escape* IVAN*'s grip, dragging him over to* LOCKHART.

SHARKY (*shouting at* LOCKHART). Come on! You and me! Outside! Let's finish this for once and for all!

IVAN. Come on, Sharky. Come on . . .

IVAN *bundles* SHARKY *towards the kitchen.*

SHARKY (*turning to shout at* LOCKHART). You fucking bastard!

IVAN *gets him into the kitchen and shuts the door. We hear* SHARKY*'s muffled cries for a moment and* IVAN*'s soothing voice.*

LOCKHART. What did I do?

RICHARD. No, no, Mr Lockhart, you didn't do anything. What did any of us do, sure? I can only say I'm terribly sorry . . . for his behaviour . . .

LOCKHART. Not your fault, Richard.

NICKY (*picking up an overturned chair and a glass*). He's renowned for that temper. Renowned. He can't drink! He never could! He's barred out of . . . Richard?

RICHARD. Ah, he's barred out of nearly everywhere. He can't even get a job on the fishing boats anymore . . . They won't have him.

NICKY. Yeah! Like, he had a go at all of us there! You know what I mean?

RICHARD. That's what I live with! That's what we all had to live with, with him.

NICKY *shakily pours them all a drink.*

If our poor old ma said left, Sharky said right. If our Da said up, Sharky went down. They'd send him out on a message, maybe to get a few bottles of stout or whatever, he just wouldn't come back! He was like a stray cat in a sock, God help him. Always. And you also have to excuse that he hasn't had a drink in a couple of days, Mr Lockhart. And I don't know why he bothers. That's like running into a brick wall at full tilt there now tonight again, the fucking eejit . . . What's he drinking?

NICKY. He's drinking that fucking poteen shite you got from the North!

RICHARD. Yeah, I should have known . . . But, this is the mad thing, he'll be grand now in a minute, watch! Won't he, Nicky?

NICKY. Oh yeah, he'll calm right down now, wait till you see . . . I should probably be heading on soon anyway or we won't get a taxi . . .

RICHARD. Ah, Nicky . . .

NICKY. Fucking . . . Sharky's left hook is nothing compared to Eileen's, I'll tell you!

RICHARD. She wouldn't hit you, Nicky . . .

NICKY. It's the force of her words, Richard! Fucking pin you up against the wall . . .

They laugh. The kitchen door opens and a sheepish SHARKY *appears with* IVAN. *They are both holding cans of beer. Pause.*

SHARKY. I'm sorry, Nicky.

NICKY. Yeah, no worries, Shark . . .

Pause.

SHARKY. I'm sorry, Richard.

RICHARD (*grandly*). Apology accepted.

They are silent while the wind continues to blow outside. SHARKY *stands near his chair.* NICKY *sits,* IVAN *sits . . .*

Are you not going to apologise to Mr Lockhart?

Pause.

LOCKHART. No need. No need. No need.

RICHARD. No, Mr Lockhart, I think he should . . .

LOCKHART. No, no! I perfectly understand. It was only the old drink talking. Sure I'm full of it myself. I'll tell you what: the only reparation I'd require, if no one objects is . . . let's all finish up like friends and play the last hand and we'll call it a night. How does that sound?

NICKY. Good idea!

IVAN. Ah, I don't know if maybe this is such a – (*Unsaid 'good idea'.*)

NICKY. Yeah! It's alright for you there with a big pile of money in front of you!

RICHARD. No, no, don't worry, Nicky, we'll play, we'll play, won't we? Sharky? A last hand now and no digs flying, alright?

Pause.

LOCKHART. Okay, Sharky?

SHARKY (*looking at* LOCKHART). Okay . . .

RICHARD. Will someone pour Sharky a drink there, calm him down . . .

IVAN. He has one . . .

LOCKHART. Will I deal?

He expertly shuffles the cards like a dealer in a casino.

RICHARD. Fire away, Mr Lockhart!

LOCKHART. I'll give'em a good shuffle . . .

NICKY. You alright, Shark?

SHARKY *nods.*

I'm sorry as well, OK?

He offers a handshake. SHARKY *shakes his hand, watching* LOCKHART *shuffle.* NICKY *and* IVAN *put two euros each in the pot.*

RICHARD. He's grand! Leave him alone. I live with that silence!

LOCKHART (*proffering deck to* SHARKY). Cut the deck, Sharky?

A little pause before SHARKY *leans forward and taps the deck with his knuckle to indicate that he is satisfied with the cut.*

(*Taking the cards and dealing.*) Right!

RICHARD. I feel a big win in me waters!

NICKY. That's my big win!

RICHARD. Then why am I feeling it in my waters?

NICKY. Your waters is warning you.

RICHARD. Oh, I don't know about that. I heard a little whistle from Santy down the chimney, Mr Lockhart . . .

LOCKHART. Well, last hand! I feel something's really gonna happen . . .

NICKY. Something's got to give . . .

They all collect their cards and peruse them.

Well . . .

RICHARD. Anything interesting, Nicky?

NICKY. A card or two of note . . .

RICHARD. Ivan?

IVAN. We're doing alright . . .

LOCKHART. Care to open the betting, Ivan?

IVAN. Ah, last hand, we'll open it with five euros.

He puts five euros in the pot.

NICKY. Five euros?

RICHARD. Easy now, Ivan!

NICKY. Here, wait! Who's shy?

SHARKY. Oh, sorry . . .

SHARKY puts two euros in the pot . . .

LOCKHART. I'd hate for you not to be in this hand, Sharky.

SHARKY. Yeah . . .

RICHARD. So five to play, lads.

NICKY. I'll hang around.

He puts in a fiver.

LOCKHART. Sharky?

SHARKY considers . . .

Ah, you're not gonna go without a fight?

RICHARD. Sharky's had more than enough fights! You should sit this one out, Shark, hang on to your few shekels and don't have me be bailing you out . . .

LOCKHART. Ah, it's the last hand . . .

RICHARD. Exactly!

SHARKY. No. I'm in. (*He puts in five and then throws in another note*). With twenty.

The table reacts.

RICHARD. With what? Twenty? You fucking berk!

NICKY. Ah, now, here! Hello . . .

RICHARD. What are you doing?

IVAN. Let him play, Rich . . .

RICHARD. Ah, this is mad! How are we doing? What have we got?

IVAN leans over to confer with RICHARD, whispering in his ear.

NICKY. God, Shark! I thought we were quits . . . the punishment continues!

LOCKHART. It's only a game!

NICKY (*sarcastically*). Oh, is it?

LOCKHART. Are you in or out, Nicky?

NICKY. Ah fuck it, come on!

He puts in twenty euros.

LOCKHART. Ivan?

IVAN. We'll see it . . .

LOCKHART. And so will I.

IVAN and LOCKHART put in twenty.

RICHARD. You're some bollocks, Sharky.

IVAN. Let him play, Dick.

LOCKHART. Ivan?

IVAN (*throwing a card in*). Just one please, Mr Lockhart.

LOCKHART. One . . .

He deals him a card.

NICKY (*incredulous*). One?

RICHARD. Yes, Nicky, one.

LOCKHART. Sharky?

SHARKY. One.

NICKY (*downbeat*). One as well?

RICHARD. Ah, he's having a laugh, don't mind him.

NICKY. And what are yous doing?

RICHARD. We're not messing about. We're playing for keeps.

NICKY. Great . . . Give me three.

LOCKHART (*dealing him three cards*). Three.

NICKY *looks at his cards.*

RICHARD. That made you go quiet.

NICKY. No, it didn't.

RICHARD. What suddenly happened?

NICKY. No, nothing . . .

RICHARD. Go on out of that. Nicky suddenly has a hand.

NICKY. Why don't you play me and find out. With your
pathetic little run up to a six or whatever it is.

RICHARD. Don't worry, we will. How many did you take,
Mr Lockhart?

LOCKHART. I'm happy.

NICKY. You're happy?!

LOCKHART. No cards. I'll stick with these.

NICKY. Oh bollocks.

LOCKHART. The bet's to Sharky.

RICHARD. Throw 'em in, Shark. Don't lose it all on a bluff
now.

Pause. SHARKY *considers* LOCKHART.

SHARKY. Fifty.

NICKY. Oh God . . .

RICHARD. Sharky!

IVAN. No, let him play, Dick!

LOCKHART. Nicky?

NICKY. Oh God . . .

NICKY *gets up and walks away from the table.*

RICHARD. Where's he going?

NICKY. I'm thinking!

RICHARD. God help us!

Pause. NICKY *comes back, taking some money out of his pocket.*

NICKY. Come on! It's Christmas. Fifty. I'm in. And I'm fucked now.

LOCKHART. Ivan?

NICKY. Sure he (*Sharky*) has nothing.

IVAN. Yeah. (*He puts in fifty.*) Fifty.

RICHARD. Jaysus, you're very *flathulach* (*Irish for 'generous'*) with my money there now, Vano.

IVAN. Hey, I won some of this too, Rich, don't forget.

RICHARD. Yeah well, easy come . . .

LOCKHART. And I'll see Sharky's fifty. With fifty.

NICKY (*throwing in his hand, then standing up*). Ah here! If yous are . . .

RICHARD. With what?

IVAN. With fifty . . .

NICKY. 'Cause if yous are . . .

RICHARD. With fifty?!

IVAN (*trying to keep* RICHARD *committed*). No, hold on . . . hold on . . .

NICKY. This is just too expensive! I mean I can have fun for nothing, like!

RICHARD. You out, Nicky?

NICKY. I'm gone! I'm out . . .

NICKY *goes and grabs his jacket.*

(*Almost mumbling.*) This is fucking crazy . . .

LOCKHART. Ivan?

IVAN *turns to whisper to* RICHARD. SHARKY *sits watching* LOCKHART, *who returns his gaze.*

NICKY. Lads, I have to shoot. 'Cause we won't get a taxi . . .

RICHARD. Yeah, hold your horses . . .

NICKY. Yous have all me money!

RICHARD (*to* IVAN). Go on, go on . . .

IVAN. We're in.

He puts in fifty.

NICKY. Jaysus . . .

LOCKHART. Sharky.

SHARKY. Here. (*Raising.*) And whatever else this is . . .
  eighty . . .

LOCKHART. With eighty?

RICHARD. Sharky, what are you doing? You mad bollocks?

LOCKHART. Ivan?

NICKY. Lads . . . don't blow a good evening now . . .

IVAN. No, we'll see it . . .

RICHARD. Ivan . . .

IVAN. To you, Mr Lockhart.

LOCKHART. Well, I've no change so I'll just throw in a
  hundred.

IVAN. So twenty to play.

He puts in twenty to see the bet.

RICHARD. Ivan!

IVAN. We're alright, Dick.

RICHARD. Speak for yourself!

LOCKHART. Sharky?

SHARKY. Em . . .

NICKY. Sharky's busted. You're gone, Shark, you're out . . .

LOCKHART. Well, if he wants to play . . . I know he's good for it.

RICHARD. Good for it?! He is not!

SHARKY. Richard, I have it.

RICHARD. Where? Under the mattress down in Lahinch?

SHARKY. Yeah, just not . . . I have it.

RICHARD. Where?

NICKY. Ah, he's good for it, Rich.

LOCKHART. I'll play him.

RICHARD. What the fuck is this, the Credit Union? Sharky, if we win, you've to cook that coddle I been asking you for, right?

SHARKY. Yeah, alright, I'll do it!

RICHARD. With the black pudding?

SHARKY. Yeah, alright!

NICKY. He'll do it . . .

RICHARD. Yeah, but what if Mr Lockhart wins? Who's gonna pay him for Sharky?

SHARKY. I'll pay him myself.

RICHARD. With what?

IVAN. We'll give it to him!

RICHARD. We'll have nothing left!

LOCKHART. We'll go up to the hole in the wall, sure. Isn't there one up there by the off-licence?

RICHARD. The hole in the wall? (*Laughing.*) Sharky has no bank account!

SHARKY. I have it, Rich, alright? Just let me play.

RICHARD. Do you have a sneaky bank account? Are you putting all my change from the shopping in there?

SHARKY. Richard! Would you give it a rest?

RICHARD. You're gone mad!

LOCKHART. I'm happy to play him, Richard. And I'm happy to go up to the hole in the wall with him if I win.

IVAN. Let him play, Rich . . .

RICHARD. Okay! But this is . . . I give up. I fucking give up!

LOCKHART. So? We're all in? Show our hands?

NICKY. Yous probably all have nothing, have yous?

Pause. SHARKY *takes a long drink.*

LOCKHART. Sharky?

SHARKY. I have a poker. Four eights.

SHARKY *and* LOCKHART *sit watching each other.*

NICKY. Four fucking eights? Bang!

IVAN. Yous are not gonna believe this . . .

RICHARD. I'm sick . . .

NICKY. What have you got, Ivan?

IVAN. We had a poker as well! Four fours!

RICHARD. Ah, this is a disaster!

NICKY. No!

IVAN. Four fours . . .

He throws his cards face down with disgust . . .

NICKY. Sharky wins! What a hand, though! Both of yous!

RICHARD. That is a total killer now . . .

LOCKHART. Well, one moment gentlemen, please . . .

Pause. He lays his hand down for them to see. SHARKY *closes his eyes when he sees it.*

NICKY. Four tens!!! What are the chances?!

RICHARD. What?

IVAN. Four tens . . .

NICKY. Sharky . . .

RICHARD. Did Sharky blow it?

NICKY. Sharky, you're beaten . . .

RICHARD. Sharky, you fucking eejit!

NICKY. You had to play it.

RICHARD. What were you doing?

IVAN. He had to play with a hand like that, Dick, come on . . .

RICHARD (*angrily*). Ah!

NICKY. Well you certainly cleaned us all out, Mr Lockhart.

LOCKHART. A pleasure, gentlemen . . .

IVAN. Hard luck, lads . . .

NICKY. Look, I'm gonna have to see if I can grab a taxi. (*Remembering he is broke.*) Eh . . . D'you want to share one, Mr Lockhart?

LOCKHART (*rising, collecting his money*). No, I'm going to walk, Nicky.

NICKY. All the way up to Howth?

LOCKHART. I always like to savour the last few hours of dawn before the Child arrives. I never have too long, you see. Sharky'll keep me company as far as the hole in the wall anyway.

NICKY (*baffled*). Eh . . . well, whatever you want . . . I'm gonna . . .

He zips up his jacket.

LOCKHART. Sharky?

SHARKY. Yeah.

RICHARD. Here, take it from me, Mr Lockhart, what do we owe you, twenty?

SHARKY. Nah, it's alright, Dick, I'll go with him . . .

RICHARD. But we have it here! Give it to me later!

SHARKY. Nah, I should give him my own . . . what I owe him.

RICHARD. Don't be ridiculous! It's the middle of the night!

SHARKY. No, it's fine. Really . . .

RICHARD. Talk about contrary! Sharky, come on . . .

NICKY. Here, Ivan, do you want a lift if I can grab a taxi out on the street?

IVAN. Oh, I don't know if I'd be welcome now at this hour . . .

NICKY. Would you not chance it? What time is it? It's a quarter to seven?! Oh bollocks!! How did that happen?

IVAN. What? Oh God, okay, let me have a slash quickly!

IVAN jogs into the kitchen to use the toilet. NICKY runs up the stairs.

NICKY. I'll see if I can grab a jo. I doubt it though . . . Bollocks!

He is gone.

LOCKHART. Well, Richard. It was very nice to make your acquaintance.

RICHARD. Yes! Well, thank you for calling.

LOCKHART. I hope you're not too sore about losing.

RICHARD. No, I'm just annoyed that I can't see and I can't play properly for myself. Or do anything that I'd really want. But we must do it again. Are you around?

LOCKHART. Oh I'll be gone now . . . till Good Friday anyway.

RICHARD. Well, maybe around then. And please excuse my brother and his . . . behaviour. Please, let me give you the twenty euros. I'm nervous about him going off out now at this hour . . . I just . . . he's had a few drinks and you've seen that he can be . . . Sure, you'll nearly have to go all the way up to Sutton Cross! The cash machine at the shops has been empty for days now coming up to Christmas!

LOCKHART. I'd be happy to oblige you, Richard. But Sharky seems to feel he should pay me himself.

RICHARD (*groping for money, holding out whatever he has grabbed*). Jaysus, Sharky, I'll give it to you, alright? Happy Christmas, okay? Are you happy?

SHARKY. I have to go, Richard. I have to do it myself. I'm sorry.

RICHARD. Ah, I give up! Come straight back now, won't you?

Pause.

You promise me?

Short pause.

SHARKY. Yeah.

NICKY *reappears, coming down the stairs.*

NICKY. Where's Ivan? Is he coming? I have a jo! It's Mungo Mickey's brother, whatshisname . . . He's on his way home, so come on! Ivan!

IVAN *reappears from the toilet, wearing a big pair of spectacles.*

IVAN. I found me glasses!

RICHARD. Well thank fuck for that!

NICKY. Come on, do you want to chance it, I'll bring you home?

IVAN. Oh, I don't know . . . I'm really after blowing it now sure, it's the fucking morning!

RICHARD. Look, hang on here with me, Ivan, we'll give her a ring, alright? And smooth the passage . . .

IVAN. Yeah, maybe . . . (*Defeated.*) Oh . . . Sure, I'm jarred, Nicky . . .

NICKY. Okay, well, look, I'll see yous. Good luck, Richard.

NICKY comes and shakes hands with RICHARD. IVAN sits at the table and takes a drink.

RICHARD. See ya, Nicky, me old flower!

NICKY. And I'll be in to see you now over the Christmas. And we'll have a nice, proper Christmas drink . . .

RICHARD. Absolutely. You'll have to rescue me.

NICKY. Would you go on out of that, you don't need rescuing, Dick! (*Hurrying towards stairs.*) Lads, I'll see yous. You sure yous won't take a lift?

IVAN. Here, hold on . . .

He picks up his hand from the game . . .

These is four aces!

NICKY. What? (*He goes to look.*) It is! Yous had four aces, you dozy fucking eejit!

RICHARD. What's he saying?

NICKY. Yous had four aces!

IVAN. I thought they were fours, I couldn't . . .

NICKY. Yous won it! (*Turns to* LOCKHART.) They beat you, Mr Lockhart . . .

LOCKHART. No . . .

NICKY. No, they did.

LOCKHART. Let me see . . .

NICKY brings the cards to LOCKHART.

IVAN. I thought they were . . . you see I fucking thought they were fours! They were aces!

RICHARD. Well, Happy Christmas!

IVAN. I just couldn't see them!

RICHARD. Here, hold on, how many other hands did you balls up on me?

NICKY. Well, that saves you an auld trip to the hole in the wall, Sharky . . .

SHARKY *and* LOCKHART *look at each other.*

RICHARD. Let's have a drink! I knew that hand was ours! I could feel it in me waters! I told yous! Woo hoo!

IVAN. I'm sorry about that, Mr Lockhart . . .

NICKY. Oh that's a pain in the hole, Mr Lockhart. Lads, I have to run, I can't believe none of yous is coming with me! Come on, Mr Lockhart, you might as well take a lift now . . . Come on!

LOCKHART *stands there looking at them, then he takes the money from his pocket and puts it on the table.*

LOCKHART. Well, what can I say? Somebody's done you a big favour, Sharky.

RICHARD. Hey, this is a square house, there's no cheating or favours being done when it comes to playing cards in here!

LOCKHART. I'm not saying it was anyone here . . .

RICHARD. What in the name of God are you talking about? It was just a mistake. People make mistakes, Mr Lockhart. It's not the end of the world . . .

LOCKHART. No . . .

IVAN. I just couldn't see! They looked like fours . . . I didn't look at them properly, I'm sorry.

RICHARD. Hey, you owe me that twenty euros now, Sharky.

NICKY. Come on, Mr Lockhart, I'll drop you at Sutton Cross, you can stroll up from there. Sharky. I'll see you, right?

SHARKY. Yeah, I'll see you, Nicky.

They shake hands.

NICKY. Call in over the Christmas, say hello, won't you?

SHARKY. Yeah.

NICKY. Good man. Ivan, I'll see you up in Doyles no doubt, have a good one, right?

IVAN. Yeah. Cheers, Nicky.

NICKY. And don't spend all that wonga until you get me a pint of Miller, or three, right? I'm gone! Come on, Mr Lockhart, if we lose this lad we're goosed!

NICKY *runs up the stairs.*

LOCKHART. Well then . . . I'll say goodnight.

RICHARD. Yeah, good morning! Happy Christmas! I hope Santy brings you what you want!

LOCKHART (*buttoning up his coat*). I only want what yous fellas have.

RICHARD. Yeah? What's that, then?

LOCKHART (*putting on his hat*). Peace of mind.

RICHARD *and* IVAN *burst out laughing.*

RICHARD. What? Are you fucking joking me?

LOCKHART. No. Goodbye, Richard. Goodbye, Ivan. See you again.

IVAN (*pouring a drink for himself and* RICHARD). Yeah, good luck.

LOCKHART. Goodbye, Sharky.

SHARKY *doesn't answer him.*

Perhaps we'll play again some time, when my luck changes. Or yours does.

SHARKY. Nah, you're alright.

RICHARD. Sharky!

SHARKY. I just don't want to play anymore.

LOCKHART. Well you should think about it. Somebody up there likes you, Sharky. You've got it all.

LOCKHART *unsteadily mounts the stairs and goes off. The light under the Sacred Heart blinks on. The first rays of dawn are seeping into the room. The front door slams.*

RICHARD. Well Jaysus! That is one maudlin fucker! Talk about a poor loser!

IVAN. Where do I know him from?

RICHARD. Ah, he's one of Nicky's strays. Jesus Christ, it's freezing in here!

SHARKY. Yeah, let me just . . .

SHARKY *goes to the stove and puts fuel in.*

RICHARD. Good man, Sharko! Hey, do yous know what we should do? The monks do have an early mass in the Friary. Do yous feel like it? Because then – this is brilliant – we'll get one of them to run you up home, Ivan, soothe Karen's temper – they love her up there – and be an honest broker. How's that for genius?

IVAN (*considers, not too convinced*). Well, I don't know . . .

RICHARD. And you know of course that they brew their own ale up there? I was there when they started doling it out one Christmas. It's strong stuff. Two or three jugs of that after mass and you'll be whistling Dixie for the whole afternoon! What do you think, Sharky?

SHARKY. Yeah, I suppose we could walk up if it's not still raining . . .

RICHARD. Hey, Sharky . . .

SHARKY. Yeah?

RICHARD. Go over to the tree.

SHARKY. What?

RICHARD. 'What?' he says! What, did you think I didn't get you anything? What do you think I am? An ogre? Hey, Ivan, check out bah humbug over here! Go on, Ivan, get yours as well. He knows what it is. He wrapped them for me, didn't you, Ivan?

IVAN *lets out a loud snore . . .*

SHARKY. He's having a nap.

RICHARD. Ah, leave him. Yours is there. It has your name on it. It doesn't matter. They're both the same.

SHARKY. Ah, Rich, are you serious?

RICHARD. Yeah, well you don't deserve it now after your disgraceful behaviour. But sure, it's Christmas. All is forgiven. What do you say?

SHARKY *goes to the tree and picks up one of the presents.*

Open it, you berk!

SHARKY *opens the wrapping.*

You see what it is? It's a mobile phone!

SHARKY. Oh yeah. Thanks Rich . . . it's . . .

RICHARD. Yeah, well, that old 088 you were using, sure that's practically obsolete! No one can ever get you! I just thought that if you were gonna get back to the driving or if I ever needed to . . . that I could get you, you know . . .

SHARKY. Yeah . . . Thanks . . .

RICHARD. What? Is something wrong?

SHARKY. No, I'm . . . I'm just . . .

RICHARD. Ah, buck up, will you, Sharky! I don't want the whole – (*A mocking, unfair impression of* SHARKY.) 'Aw, life is too hard and I can't take it!' off you today now, right? Do you hear me? We all know you're an alcoholic and your life is in tatters and you're an awful fucking gobshite. We all know that. But you know what? You're alive, aren't you? (*Beat.*) Aren't you?

SHARKY. Yeah.

RICHARD. So come on! Buck up now! It's Christmas day and I feel like going to mass, so go on and put the kettle on! Ivan!

IVAN *jumps.*

IVAN. What?

RICHARD. You better get a cup of tea into you, come on, we're gonna go up to mass. And see if we can get one of the monks to broker a peace deal for you. (*Going towards the stairs.*) Hey, Shark, do I have a clean shirt?

SHARKY. I left one on your bed.

RICHARD. Good man, stick on a bit of toast, will you? Ivan, you might come up and help me get a shave in a minute, is that alright?

IVAN. Yeah, no problem, Dick.

RICHARD (*going up*). Hey lads, we really showed that fucker, didn't we?

IVAN. We sure did.

RICHARD. There was funny smell off him. Get Ivan a bit of breakfast, will you, Sharky?

SHARKY. Do you want a bit of toast, Ivan?

IVAN. Oh, I don't think so. I don't think I'm quite there yet.

SHARKY. Well, I'll put the kettle on.

RICHARD (*as he disappears*). Good man, Sharky. That's the way.

SHARKY *goes to the kitchen.* IVAN *wanders over to the stereo. He takes a CD from* SHARKY's *gift parcel. Morning is really beginning to pour in now. The wind has died down. The sky is clear.*

IVAN. Hey, Shark! She has good taste, your one who sent you these . . .

SHARKY *comes out with a tray, tidying up.*

SHARKY. What's that?

IVAN. No, I said you got some good music off your friend down the country.

SHARKY. Yeah?

IVAN. Yeah. These are classics.

SHARKY. Stick one on.

IVAN. Will I?

SHARKY. Yeah, go on . . .

>SHARKY *continues to tidy up while* IVAN *puts on a CD.*
>*John Martyn's 'Sweet Little Mystery' begins to play softly.*
>IVAN *stands nodding his approval in time with the music*
>*and then goes off up the stairs to help* RICHARD.
>SHARKY *pauses for a moment. He reaches into his pocket*
>*and takes out the card he received in Act One. He stands*
>*there reading, and as John Martyn sings the sunlight seems*
>*to stream in brighter and brighter for a moment, before it*
>*fades away with the music.*
>
>*End.*